LIGHTWEIGHT
DMUS

The Early Derby Works and Metro-Cammell Units

Evan Green-Hughes

Ian Allan
PUBLISHING

First published 2012

ISBN 978 0 7110 3463 1

Published by Ian Allan Publishing

an imprint of Ian Allan Publishing Ltd, Hersham, Surrey, KT12 4RG

Printed by Ian Allan Printing Ltd, Hersham, Surrey, KT12 4RG

Code: 1201/B3

Visit the Ian Allan website at www.ianallanpublishing.com

Front cover: Less than a week after the start of railcar services in the Birmingham area, on 10 March 1956, two of the new units are seen at Four Oaks station, providing a complete contrast to the dingy steam-hauled stock stored in the background. *E. S. Russell, Colour-Rail*

Back cover top: Most of the Lightweight units built by Metro-Cammell were employed in East Anglia. One of them approaches Aldeburgh station, the terminus of an 8.5 miles branch from Saxmundham with a train from Norwich, just before the line closed in June 1956. *Evan Green-Hughes collection*

Back cover bottom: The flat lands of East Anglia proved ideal for the Metro-Cammell lightweights, one of which heads for Norwich with the Driving Trailer leading. *Evan Green-Hughes collection*

Title page: The scenery on the Blaenau branch was ideal for passengers to view from the end windows of the Lightweight units. A Llandudno-bound service calls at Glan Conway with a train from Blaenau Ffestiniog. *Colour-Rail*

This page: The driver releases the brakes of his set and starts his run to Harrogate from Leeds Central on 16 June 1954. *W. S. Garth/Rail Archive Stephenson*

Contents page: The railway to which the Lightweights were introduced was still essentially as it had been before the war, as can be seen by this view of Bicester (London Road). The unit is showing a red light by the use of a lens over the centre marker light. *Colour-Rail*

Contents

Background

After the initial allocations 'Yellow Diamond' units tended to be moved round the country and grouped at specific depots. Driving trailer M79646 was originally allocated to the Birmingham No 1 scheme, then moved to Macclesfield, and finally to Carlisle, where it spent the last four years of its active life. While allocated to Macclesfield it is seen working a Manchester-Hayfield service at Marple Wharf Junction on 5 February 1964.
John Clarke

The years after the Second World War found Britain's railways in a very poor state. Construction of new rolling stock had been largely on hold throughout the hostilities and maintenance had suffered, partly due to facilities being given over to war production, but also as a result of higher mileages being operated by heavier trains.

The poor physical condition of the system was mirrored by the financial state in which it found itself. Losses were on a gigantic scale, with many lines failing to cover even their basic running costs; even many of the major routes were losing money. Recruitment and training of suitable staff was also becoming an issue, with many finding the poor working conditions surrounding steam engines unacceptable. Wages were low and people whose horizons had been widened by the recent conflict were all too ready to move on to better-paid jobs with better working conditions.

British Railways had been nationalised in 1948, a process which led to a countrywide cohesive management organisation being put in place, and this in turn led to a review of most railway activities, including the provision of new rolling stock. As early as August 1949 the Railway Executive set up a committee to look into the matter of traction, and this committee was instructed to examine the future possibilities of steam, electric, diesel-electric, diesel-mechanical and gas turbine motive power.

One issue that came onto the table for debate was the provision of suitable rolling stock for branch and secondary lines. Traditionally these had been worked by pensioned-off coaches from other routes hauled by steam traction, requiring a crew of at least three people. However, in many other European countries small diesel railcars were used for such work, requiring a crew of only two people, which considerably reduced operating expense. At this time there were also two private companies anxious to try similar products in the UK, namely Metropolitan Railcars (Ganz), which was offering a version of its German railcar, and ACV, which was building a train of four-wheel railbuses for evaluation.

In June 1951 the Executive agreed that Mr M. G. Bennett, Superintendent of the Operational Research Division of the Executive's Research Department, should look into the matter, together with regional representatives, and that they should consider input from Robert Riddles, a member of the Railway Executive for Mechanical & Electrical Engineering who would submit proposals for steam push-pull trains; from Messrs ACV, which had a four-wheel diesel unit in development; from the Western Region, which already had considerable experience with railcars; and from the Eastern Region, which had had a fleet of Sentinel steam railcars. By August the Executive was reporting that it would be difficult to 'stand aside' from development of the diesel railcar as the matter was being given considerable attention by other railway administrations.

Consequently in September 1951 a Light Weight Trains Committee was formed under the chairmanship of H. G. Bowles, Assistant Chief Regional Officer of the Western Region, and including his counterparts from the Eastern (A. J. White), the London Midland (E. S. Hunt) and the Southern (S. Wymer). Other members were M. G. Bennett and the Executive Officer of the Passenger Railway Executive, L. W. Conibear. The secretary was F. G. Richens, who was secretary of the Western's Chief Regional Office.

The Light Weight Trains Committee had one simple task – to come up with proposals for replacement trains for branch-line work that would cut costs to the extent that many lines would return to profitability. Having come up with recommendations as to what form of traction was to be adopted, the Committee was to suggest a number of areas where their proposals could be tried out. If these experiments were successful, they would be extended throughout the network.

No time was lost in gathering information for this brief, for time was short. Within two weeks members were on their way to Ireland, where they spent a weekend with representatives of the Great Northern Railway and the Ulster Transport Authority looking at the new multiple-purpose diesel units in service there. Importantly the party was joined by Frank Pope, who had been Chairman of the UTA from 1948 to 1951, and who had then moved on to the British Transport Commission. Pope was a great advocate of the

diesel railcar and would subsequently be instrumental in the development of future policy. On the party's return, F. J. Wymer, Assistant Chief Regional Officer, Waterloo, consulted extensively with London Transport as to the reliability of the RT bus, gaining figures on miles-per-casualty and general design, which were later to prove very useful.

By November 1951, only two months after starting their work, the Committee was able to report that there would be significant financial advantages if diesel units were to be adopted for secondary services, but this did not please everyone. There were complaints that steam traction was not being given a fair hearing, but the Committee countered by saying that Mr Riddles and his team were offering nothing new. The Southern, meanwhile, was working on a proposal to fit an engine-generator set into a standard EMU, which they felt would offer advantages in maintenance.

Before another month had passed members of the Committee had paid a visit to the ACV works at Park Royal to see the four-wheelers that were under construction there, and the members then spent most of January touring Belgium, France and Germany, where they examined several different types of railcar. February saw them at the Birmingham Railway Carriage & Wagon Works site, where they were able to view a five-coach main-line and a five-coach suburban unit that the company was building for service in Egypt. As a result of all these visits the members came to the conclusion that diesel-mechanical transmission was preferable, with power available of up to 500bhp.

Only six months after beginning their work, in March 1952, and with commendable speed, the Committee published its first report. It had looked carefully at all the forms of traction offered. As far as steam was concerned, the Sentinel railcars were to be discounted in the light of unsatisfactory experiences with both those operated previously in the UK and in France and Belgium. Steam push-pull trains had certain advantages – for instance, there was no requirement for them to run round at the end of each

The Lightweights intrigued spotters and travellers alike and were immensely popular, in some cases tripling loadings over the steam services that had preceded them. Two drivers are obviously learning the ropes on this Liverpool-bound set, but unfortunately the original slide does not give us a date or location. *Colour-Rail*

A Derby Lightweight pulls up at Sandy next to a relatively new Brush Type 2. There is evidence of the considerable parcels traffic that originated in this area. *Colour-Rail*

trip – but they were dirty and costly to operate. Diesel railcars offered quick acceleration, faster point-to-point timings, either-end driving positions, greater availability and much reduced cost. In addition, the Committee concluded that the diesels were 'in line with modern conceptions and had a strong psychological appeal' and could also offer levels of comfort to rival those being offered by the road coach and the private motor car.

The report went on to examine the scope for the introduction of such trains and concluded that the best savings could be made in rural areas, while the urban traveller might be tempted back off the bus if railcars were to be adopted in some areas. However, the biggest savings were to be made in areas where traffic was light and where the best opportunity could be made of the greater distances that railcars could cover each day as against steam trains. Three schemes were therefore proposed. The first would cover an area of Lincolnshire, bounded by New Holland, Grimsby, Skegness, Grantham, Boston and Retford, where

railcars would be used on secondary passenger services. This would require 13 two-car units at a cost of £325,000. The second scheme would cover urban services around Halifax, Leeds, Bradford and Harrogate and would require eight two-car sets at a cost of £200,000. The third would cover inter-urban services between Newcastle, Hexham and Carlisle. Also included would be Carlisle-Whitehaven, Penrith-Workington, Carlisle-Silloth and Carlisle-Edinburgh. Required for these services would be 13 two-car sets, two three-car sets and ten four-car sets at a cost of £915,000. Six other schemes were also suggested, which could follow on from the first three if required.

Despite the saving claimed in the report, the steam lobby was still not convinced and there was intense pressure from those who thought that an upgraded and modernised push-pull could be the answer to returning branch lines to profit. This lobbying proved successful when the British Transport Commission considered the matter in May 1952. While accepting the Committee's recommendations and resolving

High Lane station in Cheshire was once part of the Macclesfield, Bollington & Marple Joint Railway, and in the mid-1960s was served by Macclesfield-Manchester trains, which were usually worked by pairs of Derby Lightweight units. One such train calls at the station, which was closed in 1969. *Colour-Rail*

Although the new DMUs were largely reliable, like all things mechanical they had their moments. Here a broken-down eight-car Derby Lightweight is pushed into Seaham station by a steam locomotive, in this case an ex-North Eastern 'J27' 0-6-0, on a fine day in July 1960. *Colour-Rail*

to give the go-ahead for the Lincolnshire and West Riding schemes, it was decided that the third scheme – for Cumbria – should be selected as a pilot for modernised steam push-pull working and that costs for this should be investigated and brought to the BTC by 1 July. Work on this duly went ahead. Fifteen state-of-the-art Class 2 2-6-2Ts were planned, together with 39 new coaches, 15 of which would have driving cabs. Operating costs were calculated to be 61.03d per mile, a saving of 12.88d over current costs, but this did not compare well with the diesels, which had come out at 28.10d per mile, less than half of that for steam. Finally the BTC saw sense and cancelled the steam project, saying that the experiment could not be justified on operating, commercial or economic grounds. The issue of steam versus diesel was never again referred to.

There was a further hold-up when the BTC decided to backtrack on the Lincolnshire proposals because of fears of the effects that diesel railcars might have on local bus services; these were operated by the Lincolnshire Road Car Company, a subsidiary of the Tilling Group, which was owned by the British Transport Commission. The Light Weight Trains Committee was asked to examine alternative proposals, and, in an additional report the following July, came up with an alternative scheme based on East Anglia, which had similar characteristics to that originally proposed for Lincolnshire and which would require the same number of two-car sets. However, while this was going on someone thought to speak to the bus company concerned, which had no objections to improved train services at all, with the result that both the original scheme and its replacement were both authorised on 12 November 1953.

By the end of that month, therefore, orders had been placed at Derby Works for eight two-car sets for the West Riding scheme, 13 for the Cumbrian scheme, 13 for East Anglia, and a final 13 for Lincolnshire – one more scheme than originally planned. The total cost was £1,283,936.

Even before the ink was dry on those contracts, before the first unit had entered service and before any sort of

Many of the Derby Lightweights survived long enough to receive BR's Corporate Blue livery, which began to be applied in 1964. M79144 was new to the Birmingham area but spent much of its life at Macclesfield before ending its days at Carlisle. It is wearing the original version of the blue livery, which had 3-inch-high side numbers. *Colour-Rail*

evaluation had been carried out, the BTC decided to forge ahead with more schemes. The London Midland Region identified that substantial savings could be made on its Bacup branch if it was to be allocated some of the new trains, while other Regions pitched in with ideas. Within a year of the initial orders, schemes were also approved for similar trains for Newcastle-Middlesbrough, the Birmingham area, and lines around Manchester and North Wales. As there were now many more schemes in the pipeline, this created a problem, as Mr Pope reported to the Committee in April 1954, for Derby Works just did not have the capacity to build all that was required. The answer was to prepare a general specification, which was circulated to all rolling stock builders with the necessary experience, an initial order also being placed with Metropolitan-Cammell of Washwood Heath, Birmingham, for 36 sets later the same month. These were to be the first of a large number of contractor-built sets, which, together with those built by British Railways itself, would eventually number around 4,200 and which would revolutionise travel, in the process saving a large number of branch and secondary services.

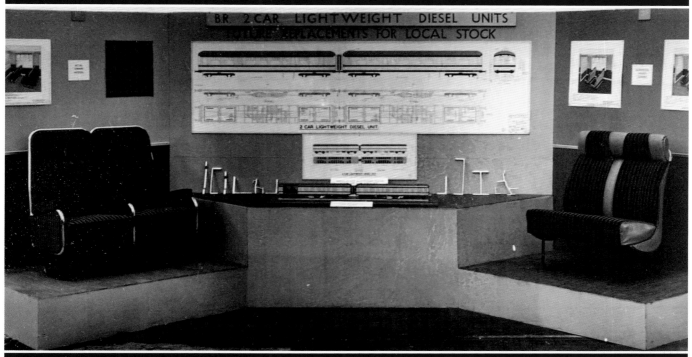

2

Development

While the Committee had sought assistance from within British Railways, it had also extensively consulted abroad and had looked at the various designs of railcar that were already in operation

However, the only real experience lay with the former Great Western Railway, whose single and two-car units had proved a great success. The GWR's successful AEC engines, married with mechanical transmission, had been very reliable. Following the war the same engine/transmission arrangement had been used in Northern Ireland, which also had experience of building railcars for its own use.

Generally speaking, Europe had much more experience with such trains. France had used diesels since 1933 and was operating more than 700 at the time the Committee was formed; these were single and twin-car diesel-mechanicals and three-car diesel-electrics. Germany was another large user, having 850 in service, ranging from four-wheeled single vehicles to express units that could cover distances of 200 miles at speeds of up to 80mph. Examinations of all these led to the conclusion that there was nothing that would be suitable 'off the peg' for British use. The Committee was, however, able to conclude that diesel engines, coupled to mechanical transmission, were to be preferred in installations of up to 500hp, with diesel-electric becoming more favourable after that point.

A number of exhibitions were held to show off designs for the new trains. Here the new seating is shown, together with some of the alloy sections. *British Railways*

In September 1952 the drawing office at Derby Carriage & Wagon was instructed to begin work on designing a suitable vehicle, based on the then standard LMS length of 57 feet and a maximum width of 9ft 2in. One early target was to find out exactly what such a vehicle was likely to weigh. These calculations revealed that, even with full integral construction, in order to meet the performance criteria demanded and using commercially available diesel engines, the new trains would have to be made of light alloy, which would save about 5 tons for each vehicle. The workshops subsequently invited ICI (Metals Division) to become involved in the design of the body structure, for up to this point the only alloy vehicles in service were 66 electric vehicles used on the Manchester-Bury route.

Certain other criteria were also specified. As early as May 1952 C. K. Bird of the Eastern Region had suggested that passengers should have a view through the ends of the vehicles. It had also been decided that each two-car unit should seat 16 1st Class and 114 3rd Class passengers, which in turn precluded mounting any of the power or transmission equipment above the solebar; even then, 3+2 seating would be required. The choice of the 57-foot underframe in turn limited the space available for the power equipment. Conventional trussing was not possible due to the presence of the underfloor equipment and the full strength of the body would have to be provided by the integral construction. Production constraints meant that the underframe, body and roof would have to be constructed as separate assemblies, with some tolerance to be allowed in the fitting of the sections.

An early arrangement drawing that exists in the official files at the National Archive shows a two-car unit with three doors on each side of each coach. Interestingly, the drawing shows only a half-cab being provided for the driver, with 1st Class forward-facing seats being arranged around it, and with allowance being made for a corridor connection to the front if required. The toilet was situated in the same area as the brake compartment, being accessed from the nearby vestibule, and there were no fewer than three sets of double sideways-facing seats in each vehicle. This arrangement would have given 16 1st Class and 124 3rd Class seats.

However, the general arrangement that was eventually agreed provided for two doors on each side of each vehicle, plus those for the driver and the guard. 1st Class was to be situated at the driving end of the trailer vehicle, while the toilet compartment was to be located at the opposite end, near the corridor connection. The brake compartment was to be in the motor car, at the opposite end to the driver's cab, and was to be fitted with double doors at each side.

Collaboration with ICI resulted in the specification of an alloy, known as Kynal M.39/2, for all main structural members and panels. This was a fully heat-treated aluminium magnesium silicon alloy having an ultimate stress of 20 tons per square inch, with an elongation of 10 per cent. All the original vehicles were made exclusively from this, but later ones sometimes used materials from other suppliers to the same specifications. The choice of this material ruled out assembly by welding because further heat would affect the stability of the heat-treated alloy, so the design was based on a riveted construction, with all rivets being of the same light alloy, cold formed in the condition in which they were received by using hydraulics. It was not, however, possible to eradicate welding altogether, and some was eventually required to the horizontal joints in the bodyside panels adjacent to the top and bottom window openings and where a flush finish was desired for aesthetic reasons.

While the design work was proceeding, Mr Riddles was authorised to invite tenders to supply the power equipment, and both Leyland and AEC submitted tenders. AEC wanted £4,625 per engine, while Leyland came out marginally cheaper, at £4,255. The decision to go with Leyland engines was not based purely on cost, however, as Robert Riddles had decided that the new railcars should be built with Leyland's torque converter transmission, which was readily available proven technology, and which would simplify the driver's controls and would be easier to maintain. Unfortunately, the Leyland system was already obsolete and was being replaced with the pre-selector on buses, while both the Great Western and the UTA had already successfully used the Wilson epicyclic gearbox, which was also later to be adopted as the standard by British Railways. It may be that Riddles was influenced by the fact that the former LMS used the Leyland system on its experimental pre-war three-car set and he was already familiar with it.

By February 1953 there was sufficient confidence in progress for authorisation to be given for the purchase of other parts that would be required, and in May £12,936 was promised for special tools to aid construction at Derby while £25,120 was allocated to the purchase of the jigs that would be necessary to assemble the new railcar bodies. Once these were in hand work commenced on the first of the body structures.

Detail design work still continued, and even as late as January 1954 Mr Eling-Smith, Derby's Chief Carriage & Wagon draughtsman, was visiting Belfast to gain experience from the new lightweight trains that the UTA was building. The North Eastern Region, which was to get the first of the new build, was meanwhile expressing doubts about the proposed timescale and asked the BTC to refrain from publicising the introduction of diesel services until matters were a little more advanced. There was another spanner in the works when the Civil Engineer responsible for the area covered by the second proposed scheme, in Cumbria, realised that he was to receive the new diesels and that they were slightly oversize for the tunnels on the Maryport & Carlisle line. Fortunately, the drawing office was able to accommodate his concerns and issued revised drawings within nine days of the matter being raised.

Away from Derby there were also many other matters to be resolved before one of the new trains could be completed. In November 1953 it was agreed that the Motive Power Superintendent would be responsible for the new trains but that the bodies would be looked after by the Carriage & Wagon Department and the electrical equipment by the Mechanical & Electrical Engineer, while a month later representatives from ASLEF and the NUR were taken to Northern Ireland to see the diesel railcars in service there, being informed of what was actually proposed during the same trip. Fortunately the union delegates could see that changes were necessary and limited their comments to requests for more information as to staffing changes at depots that were to receive the new diesels.

With design matters fully dealt with and agreement on many other fronts, it was now time for full-scale production of the country's first post-war diesel railcars.

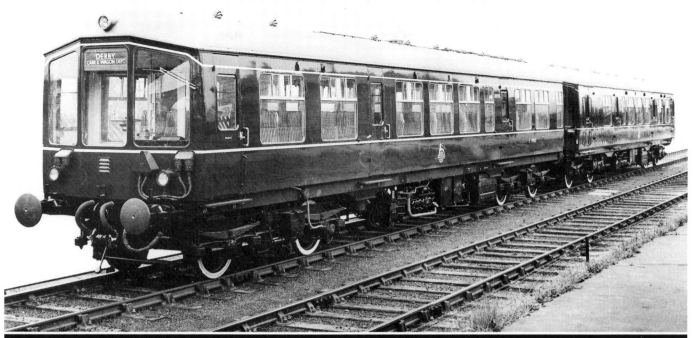

3

Construction

As might be expected with something so radically different from what had gone before, production of the Derby Lightweights was not without its problems, and it seems that a great deal of the detail was sorted out as the first build went along.

Construction started with the underframe, which was mainly assembled from standard extruded channels, angles and tee sections. Holes were then drilled for the rivets, but so that there was no slack they were drilled undersize and opened out during assembly. The bodyside frames were made using body pillars pre-formed to the correct radius and were made up on their sides. The various parts would interlock with each other, due to the design of the extrusions used.

Next the bodyside panelling was cut from 10swg sheet, with a continuous length being used between doorways above and below the windows, making some sheets around 20 feet in length. After finishing, the panels were drilled using templates, placed on the bodyside framing and the two riveted together. Roof construction followed a similar pattern.

Once the underframe was completed it was mounted on temporary bogies and taken to an area where it could be placed on jacks to give it the correct shape. There the sides and ends were fitted before another move saw the roof attached. The end canopies over the cab and the corridor connection were made from nine individual

The first completed unit was taken, as was the custom, to the Duffield-Wirksworth branch for an official photograph to be taken. British Railways, Evan Green-Hughes collection

pieces and were hand-beaten to shape by craftsman before being welded together and attached to the rest of the roof. The final operation was the fitting of the floor, which was made from extruded light alloy of an extended H section. The floor members were riveted to the underframe floor bearers and outriggers.

The interior faces of the bodyside panels were painted with bitumen to counteract condensation and all cavities between the bodyside, roof, floor, ends and interior panels were filled with sprayed asbestos. Completed body shells then moved on to be united with their mechanical components, which included air and vacuum tanks, engines, gearboxes, battery boxes, fuel tanks and bogies.

This method of construction added about £5,000 per car to the cost of construction as against conventional construction in steel, and even before the first unit had left Derby members of the Committee were raising the issue of construction costs, the matter being discussed at length in late 1953. This was probably sparked by the news that AEC now had a 150hp engine available, 25hp more than the Leylands, which would be enough to make up for the additional weight of a steel vehicle.

Workers at Derby Carriage & Wagon assemble electrical components to be fitted to the new Lightweight Trains. The vehicle in the background, 79684, was the only one allocated to the Bury services and entered service in May 1956. *British Railways*

Although the project was delivered in a commendably short time, there were problems with deliveries of raw materials that affected construction. By October 1953 production was eight weeks behind due to late delivery of light alloy extrusions, and it was reported that the engines could not be expected until the following June. In the event two did arrive from Leyland in February 1954, with a further two in March, after which they arrived at the rate of four a week. The final drives, which were coming from Walkers of Wigan, were, however, still awaited. The problems were not yet over, as some of the engines were found to be defective.

Derby Works built a prototype cab for examination by officers and staff, though the unions declined to travel from London to look at it, and at that time it was decided that the new units should be fitted with only three marker lights, as in normal running the trains would either be express passenger or local passenger and would therefore not need the centre one at the bottom. Bell communication was also ruled out between driver and guard, so was not fitted. On a positive note, all parties were able to agree on the pattern for the upholstery!

Inside, the new units were fitted with tubular steel seating trimmed with maroon moquette in 3rd Class and

Left: Assembly of the new diesel trains was a much cleaner operation than assembly of other traction units. Here workers are making up the destination indicators that would be fitted into the centre windscreens. *British Railways*

Left: Sufficient progress had been made for two of the West Riding two-car sets to work a special for railway officials, invited guests and the press on 29 April 1954. It is seen here leaving Marylebone for Beaconsfield. *Ian Allan Library*

Interestingly, it was also felt that guards should be fitted between windows and seat frames to deter pickpockets.

A second set was completed in time for a four-car demonstration run, which took place from Marylebone station, London, to Beaconsfield and back on 29 April, and this time the passengers included railway officials, invited guests and members of the press, all of whom were said to have been extremely impressed with the new trains.

Production then continued until the whole of the first batch of eight was complete. However, as there were still problems with the supply of engines from Leyland, completion was not as quick as had originally been intended, but sufficient sets had been completed by June, the start date for the West Riding scheme.

Below: The cab of the Derby Lightweight would be considered spartan by modern standards, but was positively luxurious compared to a steam locomotive. This is an early version with full-height screens. The vacuum and air gauges were mounted on the wall, rather than on the driver's desk. *British Railways*

blue in 1st. The seats were high-backed with a grab rail at the rear. The interior walls were covered in hardboard with a hard-wearing surface, and all windows were fitted with pull-down blinds.

The original order to Derby Works specified that the new trains were to be painted in BR's standard crimson and cream livery, but as the first sets came to completion the matter was considered by the Committee, which was anxious for the new trains to have an up-to-date and unique image. After discussion with the British Transport Commission during January 1954, a scheme that was described as 'GW Engine Green' was agreed on, offset by a single cream band (later amended to two cream bands). The order to Derby Works was duly amended, and the crimson and cream specification sheets were shown as 'cancelled' on 26 February 1954.

On 12 April 1954 the first set, which was the first for the West Riding scheme, was able to make a test run from Derby to Leicester and return, and eight days later the members of the Light Weight Committee were taken on a trial run. They had a number of observations on the design. They felt that the high backs to the seats spoiled the view (lower-back seats were in fact fitted after the West Cumberland batch), that consideration should be given to carpeting 1st Class, and that there should be alterations to the driver's handrails and footsteps.

Above: The first batch of Lightweights had 16 1st Class seats, while others had 9 or 12. This photo is of a West Riding vehicle, as it has no windscreen strengthening bars. Early vehicles also had square interior lights. *Ian Allan Library*

Above: 3rd Class passengers (later to become 2nd Class) were provided with high-back seating in a light and airy saloon – very different from the steam trains of the period. The seat backs were lowered from the third batch onwards. *Ian Allan Library*

E79501, seen at Beaconsfield, leads what was probably a dress rehearsal for the April 1954 press run from Marylebone. The train still has protective covers on the seats. *A. W. Croughton, Rail Archive Stephenson*

4

The West Riding sets

Within 15 months of design work being started, the first of the prototype batch of the new Lightweight trains was completed at Derby Carriage & Wagon Works.

The first batch consisted of eight two-car sets that would, it was hoped, revitalise services between Leeds, Bradford and Harrogate, where competition from municipal bus operators and difficult working conditions had resulted in a service that was losing a considerable sum of money. The new railcars cost £200,000, which it was hoped could be recouped in just four years by a combination of cost savings and by increased revenue from passengers.

The West Riding sets had made a first public appearance on 29 April 1954 when two of them were coupled together and taken from Derby to Marylebone station where invited guests and members of the press were taken on a demonstration run to Beaconsfield and back. Following that the sets were then sent north so that driver and fitter training could commence.

They were allocated to the former Great Northern Railway steam shed at Bradford Bowling Shed (later renamed Hammerton Street), which was to be their new home. This shed was crammed into a small area to the east of the city and most of the accommodation was in a multi-road dead-end building that had accumulated years of grime and peeling whitewash. Outside there were piles of ash and pits full of grime and water. No attempt was to

The Derby Lightweights were ideal for the hilly conditions in the West Riding. Here the prototype set is seen descending from Leeds Central station to Holbeck Low Level with DMBS E79000 leading. It is heading for Harrogate. Alan Earnshaw collection

be made to keep the new railcars separate from other traction at the depot, which was to prove a significant error as the units were to suffer from constant problems due to ingress of dirt and it proved difficult to keep the carriage portions clean or to carry out simple maintenance tasks adequately.

To announce the arrival of the new trains a special press run was organised from Leeds to Harrogate with the Area General Manager on board, and this nearly turned out to be a complete disaster. One of the unit's engines shut down shortly after departure, followed by a second near Harrogate. A third expired as the unit returned to Leeds, leaving the train to stagger into Leeds on its one remaining engine. The problem was traced to leaking coolant pipes, which was to remain an issue with these trains throughout much of their lives, although modifications quickly improved their reliability.

Despite this setback, the new service was launched on 14 June, the eight sets being diagrammed to take over the equivalent of 309,000 miles of steam running each year. To support the new railcars a more intensive timetable was

Right: The West Riding Lightweights can easily be identified by the different jumper cable arrangement and the lack of a bottom centre marker light. One of the batch is pictured when brand new en route to Bradford Exchange. *Colour-Rail*

introduced, providing an enhanced number of services, particularly between Leeds and Bradford. The new trains were an instant hit with the public, who particularly appreciated the clean, light and airy interiors and, of course, the views of the line ahead. The hoped-for rise in passenger numbers was almost immediate and receipts quadrupled over the next seven years.

The West Riding sets were made up of two cars, both of which were powered, in view of the heavily graded nature of the territory in which they were to work. The well-established Leyland L600 125hp horizontally mounted six-cylinder engine, as used in many buses and trucks, was specified, and two were fitted to each coach. As mentioned in the last chapter, Riddles had chosen to fit the Leyland Lysholm Smith torque converter transmission, which had been used on an earlier LMS three-car experimental unit. This had a double-acting clutch that either connected the engine output to the torque converter pump or directly to the output shaft, and was bolted directly to the engine. The clutch was controlled by the driver, who could select one

of four positions: off, neutral, converter drive and direct drive. Converter drive was used for pulling away or hill-climbing, while direct drive would be used when going downhill or when travelling along easily graded sections of track at speed. However, by the time the units were completed the Lysholm Smith transmission system was already obsolete and the buses for which it was originally designed were being equipped with pre-selector transmission.

The final drive units were placed on the inner axle of each bogie, in the centre of the axle, one of which was driven by each engine. This was again different from the Great Western's successful method of placing the final drive on the outer end of the axle, but gave the potential for much smoother operation. Involved in the development of these units were both Leyland Motors and Walker Brothers of Wigan, the latter firm having much experience of railcar development in Northern Ireland.

As the new trains were multiple units they were, of course, designed to be worked with each other, and the

Right: Only six weeks after the first Lightweights were introduced, on 8 August 1954 a set approaches the bay platform at Leeds Central with a service from Harrogate. *J. F. Oxley*

West Riding Lightweights had jumper cables permanently attached to the ends, just under the driver's window, allowing for up to eight power cars (four sets) to be coupled together and driven from the leading cab. As these sets were to remain unique in their transmission system, the jumper cables differed from later-built cars and allowed multiple working only with members of their own class. Eventually coupling codes were introduced to differentiate which types of DMU could work with each other, the eight West Riding sets being allocated the 'Red Triangle' code, which is not to be confused with the later Red Triangle code as applied to the Rolls Royce-engined hydraulic sets built for the London St Pancras-Bedford service.

With the extensive use of aluminium, including for the chassis and the ends, Derby succeeded in getting the weight of a complete two-car set down to 53 tons, which was around two-thirds of the weight of a small steam locomotive without its carriages. The heaviest vehicle was the DMBS, which came in at 27 tons, while the DMC was only 1 ton lighter at 26 tons. Sixty-one 2nd Class seats were provided in the Motor Brake vehicle, while 53 2nd Class and 16 1st Class could be found in the Motor Composite. Nine of the seats in the DMBS were to the rear of the second passenger door and were served by a large window, which was the same size as the large bodyside windows. The rather small guard's compartment relied for illumination on the light from two small windows in the doors.

A striking feature of the design was the three huge front windows fitted to the cab, which extended from the top of the driver's control desk to the roof; however, these were soon found to be weak and there were many problems with broken screens that were eventually cured by adding a strengthening bar just behind the screen and just above the driver's eye height. Problems with the riveted construction of the body soon emerged; the constant vibration from the underfloor engines caused rivets to work loose, and there were also issues with structural strength, the aluminium underframes proving particularly vulnerable to damage during rough shunting.

As the vehicles had been built at Derby Carriage & Wagon Works and, it is said, without reference to the more experienced loco works, there were problems with some of the mechanical aspects. In particular the engine water pipes and the electrical wiring were originally not durable enough for this application. However, the fitters at Hammerton Street were able to overcome most of these glitches and their work was made easier as steam locomotives were transferred away and the depot was transformed into a diesel-only shed by 1958. The old steam building was eventually replaced by a purpose-built DMU shed, and Hammerton Street then became the major DMU depot for the area.

The West Riding sets can easily be identified from other batches of Derby Lightweights as they did not have the centre marker light below the middle driver's cab window. The jumper cable receptacles were also much larger than on later builds and there were three at each end, including one purely to house the loose end of the jumper cable. Both vehicles carried the 'lion over wheel' emblem and all were painted dark green with cream lining. None survived long enough to be painted in any of the later liveries.

West Yorkshire received generous allocations of new 'Blue Square' units during the modernisation plan, including substantial numbers of Metro-Cammell and Birmingham units specially tailored to cope with the heavily graded nature of the lines in that area. This meant that the 'hydro-mech' sets were often cascaded away from their original duties and could be found on duties such as the former GNR Bradford-Wakefield service via Dewsbury and Ossett. However, as the 1960s got under way increasing competition from road

Another of the new Lightweights calls at Headingley on 8 August 1955 with a service for Knaresborough. *J. F. Oxley*

transport, as well as the closure of many lines, meant that British Railways had too many diesel multiple units in the area. This batch of Derby Lightweights was proposed for withdrawal due to their non-standard nature, and all eight were taken out of service en masse in February 1964, when slightly less than ten years old. All except 79500 were broken up by A. King of Norwich the following month; the sole survivor was broken up two years later by Cox & Danks of Wadsley Bridge, though it is unclear why this coach remained intact, as it was never used again.

Derby Lightweight West Riding sets

Numbers	Type	Diagram	Lot No	Seats	Introduced	To
E79000-7	DMBS	501	30084	61S	Apr-Sept 54	37C (later 55G) Bradford
E79500-7	DMC	507	30085	16F/53S	Apr-Sept 54	As above

E79000 was paired with E79500 and the others followed in sequence.

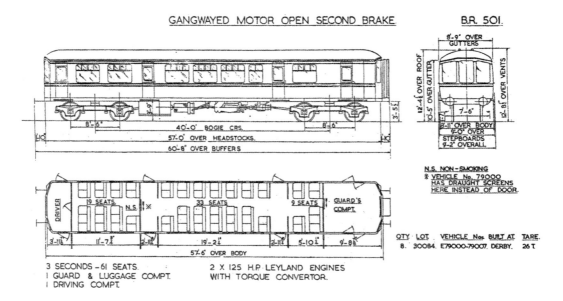

Diagram 501

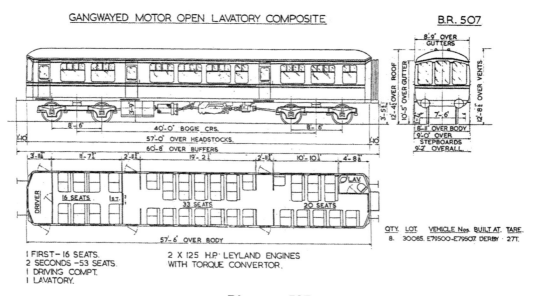

Diagram 507

Left: Maintenance conditions were primitive for the first units, which shared accommodation with steam locomotives. One of the West Riding sets is pictured at Bradford Hammerton Street shed in the company of ex-LNER 'N1' 0-6-2T No 69471. *Peter Sunderland*

Right: British Railways was so proud of its new diesel trains that it even produced postcards of them in action. This shot features one of the West Riding sets after it had been fitted with strengthening bars behind the windows. The train is displaying an oil lamp to make up for the lack of a centre marker light. *British Railways*

Left: Despite much of their work being within heavily built-up areas, the sets also worked out to Harrogate and other semi-rural areas. This train is for Bradford Exchange. *Alan Earnshaw collection*

Above: Admirers crowd round brand-new Motor Composite E79501 at Bradford Exchange station as the driver attempts to explain the brand-new technology to interested bystanders.
www.transporttreasury.co.uk

Below left: This posed shot appears to have come from official railway sources and shows the second-built Derby Lightweight at Bradford Exchange station, with an admiring driver and guard in attendance.
www.transporttreasury.co.uk

Below right: Progress in the 1950s wasn't just limited to the introduction of the new Lightweight trains. Other innovations, such as this train wash, were introduced. One of the West Riding batch of Derby Lightweights is treated to a spruce-up at Bradford's Hammerton Street depot.
www.transporttreasury.co.uk

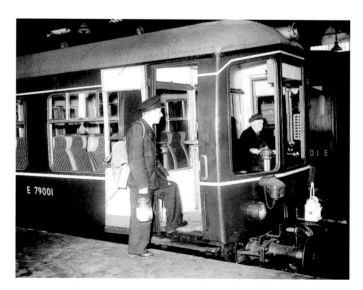

Left: Railcar mechanics were in the same league as today's computer engineers. A white-overalled technician gives instructions to a driver as one of the first units approaches Bradford. The lamp is being carried because the first batch of units did not have the centre marker lamp and therefore could not show the correct code for 'empty coaching stock'.
www.transporttreasury.co.uk

Right: Approaching Leeds Central is one of the first batch of Derby Lightweights. These two-car units had powered Composite cars, one of which is nearest the camera.
www.transporttreasury.co.uk

Left: The new diesels caused much interest wherever they went. One of the West Riding sets prepares to leave Leeds Central for Bradford Exchange on 16 June 1954, during the first week of DMU services.
W. S. Garth/Rail Archive Stephenson

21

5

The West Cumberland sets

The area selected for the second part of British Railways' diesel railcar experiment was somewhat different from the industrialised West Riding of Yorkshire, being mostly rural in nature.

The West Cumberland lines encompassed the old Maryport & Carlisle line from Whitehaven on the Cumberland coast, through Workington and Maryport and on to Wigton and Carlisle, the route southwards from Carlisle to Penrith, which used the West Coast Main Line, and the Cockermouth, Keswick & Penrith Railway from Workington to Penrith.

Thirteen two-car sets were built for these services and were delivered between November 1954 and January 1955, though by this time there had been a change of mechanical specification and this batch was to prove to be substantially different from the first. Although there had only been a couple of months' gap between the completion of the West Riding sets and those for West Cumberland, the latter vehicles were completely redesigned mechanically. The Leyland 125bhp engine had been abandoned in favour of a BUT (AEC) six-cylinder unit of 150bhp, while the outdated torque converter transmission had been replaced by the Wilson four-speed epicyclic gearbox. Also changed was the reversing/final drive on the powered axles, which was now no longer supplied by Walker Brothers but came from AEC. The engine/transmission arrangement was now very similar

Once additional units were transferred to Carlisle, DMU operation spread over a wide area. One of the original West Cumberland batch of Derby Lightweights is seen at Arten Gill Viaduct on the Settle-Carlisle line while working the 4.41pm Carlisle-Skipton service during June 1966. *Colour-Rail*

to that which the GWR had adopted for its fleet of successful railcars. The new gearbox required a change to the driving controls, and the driver's clutch/gear arrangement at his right hand was changed for a control that had four gear positions, with a separate detachable tool for forward and reverse. A clutch was not required because the gearbox automatically dealt with power input in a similar way to a bus fitted with a pre-selector gearbox.

As gradients on the West Cumberland lines were not as severe as those in the West Riding, the two-car sets were built with one coach powered and one a trailer. The engines were fitted in the vehicle that had a guard's compartment, and both coaches had a driving cab. The power cars had 61 2nd Class seats, and were similar in arrangement to the West Riding vehicles, but the trailers had only nine 1st Class seats rather than the 16 fitted to the WR vehicles. This had been achieved by fitting 2+1 seating and reducing the number of rows. Because of these changes the trailer cars weighed only 21 tons, bringing the weight of the complete two-car train seating 123 passengers down to 48 tons. Limited clearances on the Cumberland lines meant that window bars were fitted to stop people leaning out.

Maintenance of the new fleet was centred on two steam depots, Carlisle Upperby and Workington, where various modifications to the depots took place, including the installation of inspection pits, provision of new offices and a new roof at Workington. However, the Lightweights were still to be maintained beside steam locomotives and there were similar problems to those encountered in the West Riding as dirt and ash found its way into the rather more delicate mechanical portions of the new units.

Starting in October 1954, trials took place in which two of the power cars, M79008 and M79010, were used with trailer M79600 and a 28-ton coach. Various routes were tried, including Carlisle-Silloth, Carlisle-Maryport and Carlisle-Penrith, with the trains running variously as (a) Driving Motor + Driving Trailer = 55 tons, (b) Driving Motor + Driving Trailer + coach = 83.5 tons, and (c) Driving Motor + Driving Motor = 62 tons. The purpose of the test was to see if the new trains could keep to the schedules in standard form or if hauling a tail-load, and whether schedules could be improved if more power cars were used. Schedules could easily be managed with a power-trailer set, but the addition of the coach proved too much and times slipped.

Services were introduced on a gradual basis as the new railcars became available, starting with the Carlisle to Silloth branch, which went over to railcars on 29 November 1954. As more became available, services were extended to cover the whole of the Cockermouth, Keswick & Penrith section, which was well suited to railcar operation, having sparse traffic between Keswick and Penrith but high operating costs. The line also traversed some of the finest scenery in England, which could be enjoyed from the observation-like

windows of the new trains. The change, which took place in January 1955, also meant that timings could be considerably accelerated, with the 46 miles from Penrith to Workington being covered in around 1hr 10min, shaving around 15 minutes from the previous steam timetables. Some trains also worked through via Penrith and up to Carlisle. Travellers welcomed the new units, finding them clean, comfortable and efficient, and in the first few months of operation passenger numbers almost doubled when 18,500 people used the train, rather than the 10,000 who used it during the same period of the previous year.

The final phase of the Cumberland scheme was the Carlisle-Maryport-Workington-Whitehaven service, which started in February 1955. The former irregular timetable was replaced by an even-interval one, which had departures at 25 minutes past the hour from Carlisle and 5 minutes to the hour from Whitehaven, with extra services on a Saturday. Timings were again improved and 5 minutes was saved from Carlisle to Maryport, 8 minutes saved to Workington, and 12 minutes saved to Whitehaven. The response from customers was again positive and passenger numbers rose from 59,000 to 91,600.

As the West Cumberland batch of Lightweights had a different gearbox system from the West Riding cars, the arrangement of the jumper sockets was different. Each car was fitted with two sockets just below the cab windows at each side of the train and four jumper cables were provided, which were kept in lockers in the cabs. To work in multiple it was necessary to obtain four cables (two from each vehicle) and to plug them into the sockets. This proved to be a tricky

The forward view from the new Lightweight units was much appreciated in the Lake District. A brand-new set from the original West Cumberland batch calls at Bassenthwaite Lake station in April 1955. *Colour-Rail*

operation as usually only one side of the train was at a platform and the sockets were quite a stretch from the ground. The cables were completely different from those used on the West Riding trains.

In all early railcars the power to work electrical circuits, such as for gear changing and throttle advancement, came from the power car from which the set was being driven. This led to a number of problems due to voltage drop when long trains were being operated. In consequence of this, and the high-level jumper cables, these sets were later given the coupling code 'Yellow Diamond' and could only be coupled to sets similarly marked, which in practice limited them to working with other Derby Lightweights, with Metro-Cammell Lightweights and with a small batch of Cravens parcels cars.

Although this batch shared the large front windscreen with the West Riding sets, and were also fitted with a similar strengthening bar shortly after construction, they were fitted with four marker lights, rather than the three of the previous batch. This arose because the Light Weight Trains Committee had sought advice from the Operating Committee on the matter but had been unable to get a satisfactory response. Therefore in July 1954 an instruction to fit the centre marker light below the cab window was issued, presumably because with this present all headcodes shown in the Rule Book could be exhibited. Another difference from the first batch was the fitting of the bell communication system between the driver and the guard, which was done at the suggestion of the British Transport Commission.

Early on there were some problems and there was lengthy correspondence about the lack of storage in the driver's cab and whether the guard's cupboard had been incorrectly located. The British Railways Fire Department also become involved when it became apparent that when the automatic fire system was activated (this sprayed fire-suppressant gas over the engines in the event of a blaze) both engines were shut down, which could lead to the train coming to a stand at a dangerous location, such as on a viaduct or in a tunnel. A modification was ordered on all future builds, where the shut-down only affected one engine, and early sets were altered to match.

This batch of units was very successful in operation but, due to the structural weaknesses mentioned in the previous chapter and their non-standard Yellow Diamond coupling set-up, they were early candidates for withdrawal, once the full effects of the Beeching closures had taken effect. All were withdrawn between April 1967 and May 1968 and most were broken up by June 1969 by scrap-dealer Arnott Young at one of its three Scottish sites. All had worked for most of their lives on the Cumbrian lines, though one or two had been loaned for short periods to other Midland Region depots, and at the time of withdrawal all were allocated to Carlisle Upperby.

Happily, one complete set did survive to enter departmental service, this being Driving Motor Brake M79018, which became 975007, and Driving Trailer Composite M79612, which became 975008. These were used as an ultrasonic test train until the mid-1990s when they were sold for preservation. As with other Derby Lightweights, they had been insulated with deadly asbestos and this had to be removed, a considerable financial burden to the preservationists. It was carried out at Doncaster Works before the two vehicles were put into store as stripped-out shells. Following transfer to the Midland Railway-Butterley, the DMBS was subsequently fully rebuilt with funding from the Heritage Lottery Fund, the work being completed by 2007. The trailer was later rebuilt by volunteers, producing the only complete Derby Lightweight two-car set to have survived.

Derby Lightweight West Cumberland sets

Numbers	Type	Diagram	Lot No	Seats	Introduced	To
E79008-20	DMBS	503	30123	61S	Nov 54-Jan 55	12A Carlisle Kingmoor
E79600-12	DTC	509	30124	16F/9S	Nov 54-Jan 55	As above

E79008 was originally paired with E79600 and the others followed in sequence.

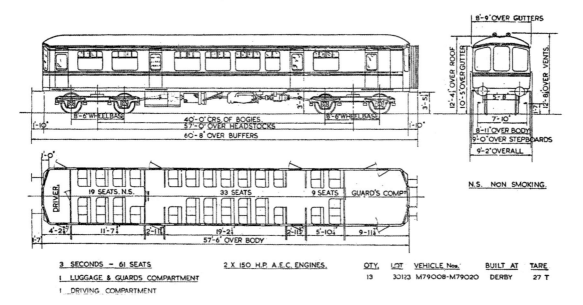

Diagram 503

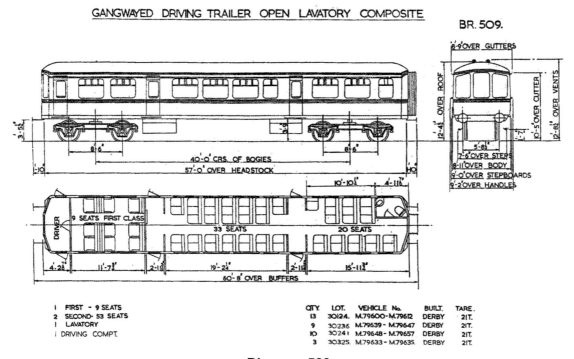

Diagram 509

Right: Later in life the West Cumberland sets received half-yellow front panels, as did many other classes of units. An unidentified member is seen at Keswick. *Colour-Rail*

Below: The Lightweights became popular for excursion work, and one of the West Cumberland batch is seen on such a duty at an unknown location in the company of an LMS Ivatt 2-6-0 steam loco. *Colour-Rail*

Right: With snow on top of the nearby mountains, one of the West Cumberland-allocated units calls at Bassenthwaite Lake station. By this time the unit has gained a half-yellow end panel and fixed jumper cables. *Ken Cooper, Colour-Rail*

Left: Pulling away from Threlkeld station, this Lightweight unit is destined for Carlisle. Together with the West Riding sets, the Cumberland units had side-mounted windscreen wipers for the driver. *Ian Allan Library*

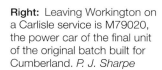

Right: Leaving Workington on a Carlisle service is M79020, the power car of the final unit of the original batch built for Cumberland. *P. J. Sharpe*

Left: One of the Cumberland batch survived to be taken into departmental use and is now the only surviving original-style Derby Lightweight, being preserved at the Midland Railway-Butterley. Formerly trailer M79612, renumbered DB975008 and in use as an Ultrasonic Test Train, is seen at Reading on 18 October 1982. *Alec Swain*

Above: In the mid-1960s many of the sets originally allocated to Birmingham, Manchester and North Wales were transferred to Carlisle. One of those so transferred brakes for the stop at Penrith while on a Carlisle-Keswick working. *Colour-Rail*

Right: When originally painted, the West Cumberland sets had the 'lion over wheel' transfer, rather than the later coaching stock transfer fitted. Trailer cars at first also had a side transfer, though this was removed on repainting. This set, which is heading for Workington, has meanwhile gained the 'speed whiskers'. *Colour-Rail*

Left: Trials were conducted in October 1954 to assess the performance of the West Cumberland sets with a coach as a tail-load, and this picture shows M79008 at Skipton with trailer M79600, the unit involved in the tests.
www.transporttreasury.co.uk

Below: The third of the West Cumberland units, M79010+M79617, stands in the centre road at Workington before forming a service to Carlisle on 23 July 1956.
K. L. Cook, Rail Archive Stephenson

6

The Lincolnshire sets

The Lincolnshire area was identified in the 1952 report as being one of those most suitable for conversion to lightweight diesel train operation. Containing a large number of lightly used lines that served countless small towns and villages, the economics of railway operation were already questionable and heavy savings would be required if the system was to stay open.

In October 1952 one of the GWR single-coach railcars was allocated to Boston for two weeks to see if diesel multiple units would be suitable for working trains in the area. It was tested on several local lines and had trips to Louth, Lincoln, Skegness and Grimsby. Local councillors pounced on the initiative and pronounced that the diesels would be ideal for saving threatened lines, such as that from Horncastle to Woodhall. In reply British Railways said it would be 'several years' before such vehicles were available to the area.

The 1952 report recommended that the area should see complete substitution of steam trains by diesel multiple units on the Cleethorpes-Lincoln, Grimsby-Firsby, Skegness-Firsby, Willoughby-Louth and New Holland-Barton-on Humber lines. There should also be partial substitution on a number of other services, including Lincoln-Boston, Lincoln-Grantham, Lincoln-Skegness, Lincoln-Retford, Lincoln-Shirebrook, Boston-Grantham, Cleethorpes-Retford, Cleethorpes-New

The second power car built for the Lincoln scheme, E79022, waits to leave Grantham on a service to Lincoln. John P. Wilson, Rail Archive Stephenson

Holland and Immingham to New Holland. There would be increased frequencies on all lines.

Ten units would be required, with three more to act as spares, and due to the flat nature of the countryside power/trailer sets were envisaged. Eighteen train crews would be displaced from their work and the scheme would save £120,640 per year.

Although the Lincolnshire scheme came high on the Committee's list of priorities, it did not find favour with the British Transport Commission. The problem, as already mentioned, was that the BTC saw it as having a detrimental effect on bus services in the area, which were operated by the Lincolnshire Road Car Company – owned by the British Transport Commission. As a result the Committee was asked to suggest an alternative area; in a supplementary report of July 1953 it proposed a scheme based on East Anglia, which was similar in nature to that already proposed and for which the proposed stock would be suitable.

However, not to be deterred, someone in British Railways organised a meeting with the management of the Tilling Group (which owned the Lincolnshire Road Car

Company) and the Light Weight Trains Committee was told in December that there would be no objections from the bus company if the diesels were to be introduced to Lincolnshire. Therefore in November the BTC agreed to the scheme, and also to proceed with that in East Anglia, which had originally been proposed as a replacement. The cost of the Lincolnshire vehicles would be £345,946 and an order was placed with Derby Works in December.

Construction of the 13 Lincolnshire sets followed on from the West Cumberland units and the first was ready by January 1955. Mechanically the arrangement was identical and the units were equipped for 'Yellow Diamond' multiple working. There were slight differences to the bodies, however. The DMBS cars (E79021-E79033) seated 56 2nd Class passengers instead of the 61 of the West Cumberland sets. This was achieved by deleting the rows of seats just in front of the guard's compartment and replacing them with two pairs of sideways-facing seats in a small area between the second door vestibule and the guard's compartment. As a result of this the large window at each side was replaced by a smaller one. The enlarged guard's compartment also gained a small window at each side. This modification was probably necessary to cater for the larger amount of market goods and produce that were carried by trains in Lincolnshire.

The trailers (E79613-E79625) were also very similar to the Cumberland sets, although the number of 1st Class seats was raised from nine to 16 by adopting a layout that gave two rows of 2+2 facing the cab partition, then two rows of 2+2 facing each other, which had previously been used on the West Riding sets.

From this batch onwards the front end of the Derby units was changed slightly to eliminate the troublesome large front windscreens. A divider was introduced just above the driver's head height, which effectively split each screen in two and added considerable strength to the vehicle end. The windscreen wiper motor was relocated to this divider (previously it was to one side of the windscreen) and two wipers were provided, a small one above the dividing bar and a larger one below it. This batch was also the first to have the lower seat backs, which were continued for the rest of the production.

Deliveries were sufficiently advanced for the first sets to be out on test in early February 1955, and these trial runs attracted considerable interest from the local press, which was particularly keen to extol the virtues of the good views to be had by sitting in the section just behind the driver. The final set of the batch reached its new home depot of Lincoln in June 1955 and the new services were immediately introduced. By the end of the year the new units had transformed Lincolnshire services, with increased frequencies and faster services and with passenger numbers rising in response.

When less than a year old and while still allocated to Lincolnshire, one of the new Derby Lightweights is seen on 24 March 1956 while working a Lincoln-Skegness service at Lincoln. *Ian Allan Library*

By 1956 Lincolnshire was receiving the first of a flood of new units, including the highly popular units that became Class 114, and which were to become synonymous with the area. All were equipped with the later 'Blue Square' coupling system, which was incompatible with the 'Yellow Diamond'-fitted Lightweights. By 1957 the first three sets – E79021+E79613, E79022+E79614 and E79023+E79615 – had moved on to East Anglia, to 32A Norwich, where there were compatible Derby units, as well as the new Metro-Cammell sets, which were also equipped with the Yellow Diamond electrical system. Two years later the rest of the batch had followed them to East Anglia, being at either Norwich or 30A Stratford, though by 1962 almost all had arrived at 31A Cambridge.

As with other parts of the country, the 1960s saw a dramatic contraction in the number of passenger services on secondary lines. Many of the services on which these units were deployed were withdrawn, and Blue Square units made available from other closed lines meant that there was no future for these vehicles and the decision was taken to withdrawn them.

All were withdrawn between September 1967 and July 1968, with scrapping being carried out by East Anglia-based scrap merchants. The exception to this was E79033+E79625, which found itself transferred to Scotland at the end of its life, being briefly allocated to Leith Central; it was cut up with one or two others at T. W. Ward of Inverkeithing in 1968.

One trailer, E79616, was withdrawn early – presumably as a result of damage – and was cut up at Stratford Carriage & Wagon Works in March 1963.

Above: Most of the Lincolnshire units were soon transferred to East Anglia to join similar units there. E79614 is seen working a Cambridge service in virtually original condition, with its power car being still fitted with the external pipes to the engine header tank, which was originally on the roof. *Colour-Rail*

Right: One of the sets originally allocated to Lincolnshire was DMBS E79029 and DTC E79621, seen here later in its life while working a Felixstowe to Ipswich service at Derby Road. *Michael P. Jacobs*

Lincolnshire sets

Number	Type	Diagram	Lot No	Region	Set	Seats	Weight	Built	Partnered when new	Original depot
79021-79033	DMBS	504	30126	Eastern	Power-trailer	56	27 tons	Jan-Jun 55	79613-79625	Lincoln
79613-79625	DTCL	505	30127	Eastern	Power-trailer	16F/53S	21 tons	Jan-May 55	79021-79033	Lincoln

E79021 was originally paired with E79613 and the others followed in sequence.

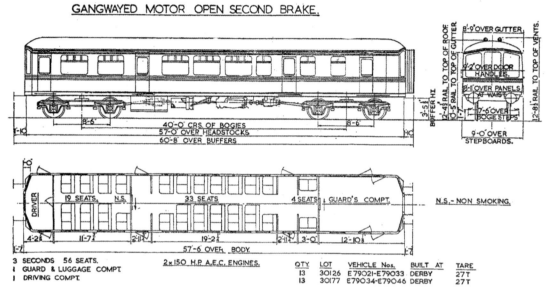

Diagram 504

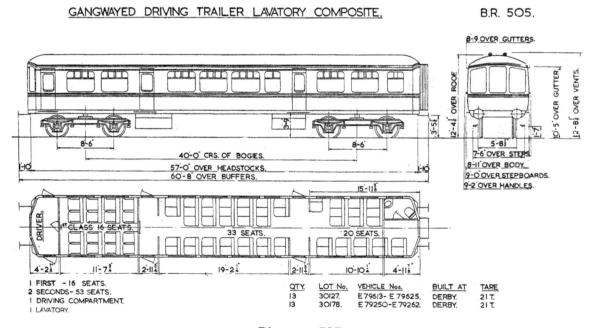

Diagram 505

Above: E79022 passes 'A1' 'Pacific' No 60117 *Bois Roussel* as it leaves Grantham on a service to Lincoln. *John P. Wilson, Rail Archive Stephenson*

Below: A Nottingham Victoria to Grantham service is seen leaving Nottingham on an unknown date, but believed to be the first day of the DMU service. E79031 is leading. *T. G. Hepburn, Rail Archive Stephenson*

Left: From the Lincolnshire batch onwards the windscreens were split and a strengthening member was put in to cut down on breakages. This can be seen clearly on this Lincoln-based unit, leaving Rauceby with a service to Grantham.
T. G. Hepburn,
Rail Archive Stephenson

Below: E79624, the penultimate trailer of the Lincolnshire batch, leads a Skegness service on leaving Lincoln Central.
T. G. Hepburn,
Rail Archive Stephenson

7

The East Anglia sets

s outlined in the previous chapter, the initial report by the Light Weight Trains Committee did not propose a scheme for East Anglia but, as a result of the intimation that the British Transport Commission would be unlikely to approve the Lincolnshire scheme, a supplementary report was published in July 1953.

This report pointed out that there were no substantial areas in the country where the issues of competing bus services did not arise – this, of course, having been the reason why the Lincolnshire scheme was to have been dropped – but, of the remaining rural areas, that centred round Norwich and King's Lynn would seem to have the most potential for modernisation.

The Committee therefore proposed that there should be complete replacement of steam trains with railcars on the Norwich-Wells and Dereham-King's Lynn services, with the diesels replacing steam on stopping services between Norwich and Ipswich and Ipswich and Cambridge. Railcars should also be substituted on services that tied in with those in the first two categories as convenient; these included Norwich-Yarmouth and Norwich-Ely; King's Lynn to Cambridge, Hunstanton, March and Audley End; Cambridge to March, King's Lynn, Colchester and Audley End; Bartlow to Audley End and Ipswich to Felixstowe.

Thirteen two-car units would be required for this scheme, which was the same number as had been

Above: It looks as though the lady with the pram is going to have a struggle to get across to catch her train as the driver has pulled up his Cambridge-bound Derby Lightweight in such a fashion as to block the foot crossing. The photographer did not record the location. *Dr Ian C. Allen, www.transporttreasury.co.uk*

originally planned for Lincolnshire, and these would provide improved local services at reduced cost, regenerating traffic as they did so. Savings were estimated to be £146,993 per year and it was anticipated that traffic receipts would increase by around £32,000 on top of that. In view of the objections to the previous scheme, and the fact that again the local buses were operated by a BTC company (in this case the Eastern Counties Omnibus Company), the Committee was at great pains to point out that road facilities in East Anglia were inadequate and often the subject of public complaint.

Most of the lines concerned had poor services and the Committee proposed to improve them by using even-time departures and introducing connections between Wells and King's Lynn services at Dereham. This amounted to an increase in passenger mileage of some 24.4% with a total daily railcar mileage of 3,503. Each unit would be expected to work 318 miles per day. The figures were based on having 11 units in service and two either under maintenance or standing spare. A maintenance depot was proposed for Norwich. Tucked away near the end of the report was a proposal to reduce the number of staff working these trains from 94 to 55, with job losses coming, as might be expected, from the ranks of firemen, passed cleaners and cleaners. Fifteen steam locomotives and 64 coaches would also be displaced.

On 12 November 1953 the scheme was approved by the British Transport Commission, surprisingly together with that it was originally supposed to replace, at a cost of £331,500. The 13 vehicles followed those for Lincolnshire from the works at Derby. The Driving Motor Brakes,

numbered E79034-46, were to the same pattern as those that had been built for the Lincolnshire scheme and had consecutive numbers. They seated 56 2nd Class passengers, having the sideways-facing seats behind the second vestibule and the smaller windows to the rear of the bodysides. They were paired with Driving Trailer Composites E79250-62, which again had 16 1st Class seats and 53 2nd Class. Deliveries commenced to Norwich Depot in June 1955 and the whole batch was available by August of that year.

Services between Norwich, Dereham and Wells, together with the connecting trains between Dereham and King's Lynn, were modernised on 19 September 1955. The service changed immediately to ten trains per day between Wells and Norwich and 14 between King's Lynn and Dereham, with the same timings as previously worked by the steam trains. The diesels also appeared, as planned, on some services to Sheringham and Holt, Yarmouth and Ipswich. As with previous schemes, receipts jumped sharply, while operating costs were substantially reduced.

Largely due to pressure brought to bear by C. K. Bird, Chief Regional Manager for the Eastern Region, who lobbied hard for more railcars, the original 13 units were joined by the 13 originally allocated to the Lincolnshire scheme, starting in 1957 and with all having been transferred by 1959. The area also received a substantial number of the new Metro-Cammell cars to the same electrical specification, allowing considerable expansion of services. These included Thetford-Swaffham, Aldeburgh-Saxmundham-Ipswich, Harwich-Ipswich, Witham-Maldon, Witham-Braintree,

Below: This side-on view of DMBS E79035, the second vehicle of the original East Anglia batch, shows clearly the two-window arrangement behind the rear vestibule. The filler pipes for the original arrangement of radiator header tank can also be clearly seen. The unit is seen at Stratford on 17 April 1958.
P. J. Sharp

Number	Type	Diagram	Lot No	Region	Set	Seats	Weight	Built	Partnered when new	Original depot
79034-79046	DMBS	504	30177	Eastern	Power-trailer	56	27 tons	Jun-Aug 55	79250-79262	Norwich
79250-79262	DTCL	505	30128	Eastern	Power-trailer	16F/53S	21 tons	July-Aug 55	79034-79046	Norwich

Diagrams for Lots 504/5 can be found on page 33

Wickford-Southminster, and St Mary's-Buntingford.

In 1957 the 38 Norwich-based units covered 30 daily diagrams, six of which were strengthening diagrams for peak times. Units ran between 300 and 400 miles a day in four-day cycles, only returning to Norwich at the end of a cycle for maintenance.

The Derby Lightweights were all replaced by slightly more modern units, with 'Blue Square' electrics, themselves displaced from other line closures, and consequently most were cut up by local scrap merchants in 1968/69, though E79034-36 were briefly transferred to Leith just before withdrawal, together with E79250-52. Two of these trailers, E79250 and E79252, were then taken into departmental service and renumbered 975013 and 975014, being used as staff messrooms, at least one at Craigentinny carriage sidings. The last was broken up in 1982. The rest of the vehicles that went to Scotland were withdrawn in 1967 and cut up by T. W. Ward of Inverkeithing.

Following the withdrawal of both the Derby Lightweights and the Metro-Cammell 79XXX series vehicles, those services that remaining in East Anglia largely passed to what became the Class 101 Metro-Cammell units, which were almost identical to the earlier vehicles save for the Blue Square electrical system. These had been made available due to line closures elsewhere and were to continue to serve the area until the first of the second-generation units arrived in the 1980s.

Below: Despite the rural nature of East Anglia, market days and excursions still demanded multiple working of units. The leading vehicle is E79251, which was the second of the original East Anglia trailers and which spent almost its entire life in the area. *Dr Ian C. Allen, www.transporttreasury.co.uk*

Left: The second unit of the East Anglia batch, E79035+E79251, approaches Long Melford with the 2.01pm Colchester to Cambridge service on 21 June 1958. *K. L. Cook, Rail Archive Stephenson*

Below: East Anglia unit E79036+E79252 enters King's Lynn on 23 June 1958. *K. L. Cook, Rail Archive Stephenson*

Left: Local spotters seem very interested in the Lightweight unit calling at Long Melford on a Bury St Edmunds to Sudbury local working during 1961. *John C. Baker*

The changes to the front ends of later batches can clearly be seen, with the front windows being divided and the wipers mounted on the dividing bar. A Cambridge-bound unit calls at Haverhill on 28 April 1961. *Colour-Rail*

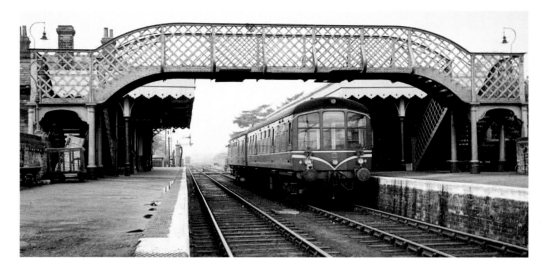

Left: The enlargement of the guard's compartment resulted in changes to the window arrangement in the East of England vehicles, with two smaller windows replacing the one larger one on each side of the compartment. This set, pictured at Mundesley-on-Sea on 20 November 1962, has also been fitted with cushioning behind the cab to protect the body during token exchanges. *Colour-Rail*

Right: Calling at Gamlingay with a Cambridge-bound service, this East Anglia-allocated set has received the modification that saw jumper cables fixed to the cab ends instead of being stowed in boxes in the cabs. *Colour-Rail*

Above: Some of the stations in East Anglia were rather larger than their potential traffic would suggest was strictly necessary. This two-car Lightweight is dwarfed by the buildings at Great Chesterford in June 1966. *Colour-Rail*

Left: Towards the end of their life some of the Lightweights were repainted in BR blue. This example must have had less than a year to go when it was pictured at Hunstanton on a Bishops Stortford working in June 1967. *Colour-Rai*

Above: There were various modifications to the units during their service life, and some lost their top marker light and/or the ventilator grille under the centre cab window (which was said to be a source of draughts). The unit working this Colchester-Cambridge service on 4 February 1967 has had both of these modifications and has only months to go before withdrawal. *P. Hocquard*

Below: A few of the Lightweights were painted in blue with full yellow ends. This four-car set with DTC E79255 leading is working the 17.52 Ipswich-Colchester service south of Manningtree on 21 June 1967, only a year before withdrawal. *G. R. Mortimer*

Left: Even though it has probably only a few months of service left, this Derby Lightweight, still in green livery, looks quite smart as it calls at Lidlington station with a Cambridge-bound train on 29 August 1967. Its trailer has been repainted in BR blue. *Alec Swain, www.transporttreasury.co.uk*

Below: A Bletchley-bound Derby Lightweight speeds past the crossing at Woburn Sands on 29 August 1967. *Alec Swain, www.transporttreasury.co.uk*

8

The Metro-Cammell cars

As plans to introduce the new diesel trains progressed it became apparent from a relatively early date that British Railways' own workshops were not going to be able to cope with the building of all the new vehicles that were likely to be required.

Only a week after the first of the West Riding sets made its test run, Frank Pope of the British Transport Commission was telling the Light Weight Trains Committee that capacity at Derby was inadequate and that what British Railways described as 'the trade' would have to be invited to tender to build some of the units required. Subsequently an eight-page specification was drawn up against which the manufacturers were to be invited to tender. The document was very loosely worded, with no specifics for power units or transmission, though 'interchangeability' with BR-built units was noted. The reasons for this lack of detail are not clear, as by this time there was a general understanding of what was required, but it may have been in deference to manufacturers such as BRCW, who had already had a great deal of experience of railcar building and who may have wished to table alternative proposals. Another possibility is that there was not general agreement among the Committee members as to what was actually required. At this stage the Eastern Region was lobbying for articulation while the Southern was not happy with the railcar concept at all, disliking almost everything, from the outward-opening cab doors to the amount of cab

Above: Pictured at Doncaster, these two Metro-Cammell units still have the delivery posters in the passenger windows. *Colour-Rail*

window glass, through to the fitting of screw couplers.

One reason that now made it possible for 'the trade' to bid for orders was the availability of 150hp engines, which meant that railcars no longer had to be built of light alloy in order to achieve an acceptable power/weight ratio. Consequently tenders were sought for vehicles to be built in steel, which gave a weight penalty of around 5 tons per vehicle but also saved around £5,000 in construction costs. Simplified maintenance and better strength were also promised.

Things moved quite quickly and the Birmingham firm of Metro-Cammell lost no time in submitting its proposals, which were rewarded with the award of an order for no fewer than 36 power-trailer sets on 1 June 1954, at a cost of £787,680. These were to be built in mild steel and were to be delivered at two to three sets a month. The BTC was evidently quite pleased with this price and was able to revise cost savings for a number of future projects based on the contract price.

One project on which the cost savings were revised was that to introduce diesel trains on the line between Bury and Bacup in Lancashire. Bury was served from a number

600 DIESEL RAILCARS

have now been supplied by

METRO-CAMMELL

for British Railways Modernisation Plan

METROPOLITAN-CAMMELL CARRIAGE & WAGON CO. LTD.

HEAD OFFICE · SALTLEY · BIRMINGHAM 8
LONDON OFFICE · VICKERS HOUSE · BROADWAY · WESTMINSTER · S.W.1

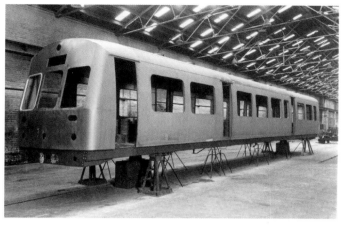

Above: An early Metro-Cammell driving trailer is seen at the Washwood Heath works undergoing deflection tests. Inside can be seen the test weights. The body has already been cut out for the jumper cables and lights. *GEC Alstom*

Above: This works photo shows the rather cramped arrangement of the power equipment under the floor of the first Metro-Cammell unit. *GEC Alstom*

Above: The interior of the Metro-Cammell units was well-designed, though there were complaints from railway officials about the size of the windows. *GEC Alstom*

of directions from Manchester, principally by electric trains from Manchester Victoria, but from there on passengers had to endure steam push-pull trains that did poor business in competition with road transport. In December 1953 members of the Light Weight Trains Committee conducted a visit to the line to see what possibilities it offered for modernisation and concluded that the line would be a suitable candidate to add to the list of lines under consideration. Initially it was assumed that the diesels would save in the order of £5,062 per year, but after the award of the contract to Metro-Cammell this was revised to £9,651. Accordingly it was agreed that the scheme should proceed as the test bed for the first of the contractor-built units, with the first seven off the production line to be allocated there.

In February 1955 the Committee received a drawing of the proposed front end of the Metro-Cammell units. This featured a sloping front end with three windows, which were much smaller than those of the BR-built units; this was not well received at all and attempts were made to get the firm to amend it, but by this time matters were too far advanced for any changes to be made. This was the first of a number of issues caused by the lack of detail in the original tender documentation, and mirrored problems suffered by other manufacturers at a later date. The BTC

Above: The driver's cab was well set out and functional, although there were worries about possible blind spots at the corners. Apart from the hinged door, the design was carried over to the later Class 101s. *GEC Alstom*

and the LWC agreed that they would prepare a joint report that would ensure that all future units complied with the standard required for appearance. This must never have been completed, for Metro-Cammell not only built all the early batch of units to this cab design, but also continued it for their numerous Class 101 vehicles that followed.

The following month there was an officers' visit to the firm's Washwood Heath premises to inspect progress when a mock-up of the offending cab was studied. This did not improve the situation, however, for it was agreed that the Derby cab was much more attractive and that the wide corners of the Metro-Cammell version might obscure the driver's vision. It was again agreed to see if anything could be done to change the design. There were also concerns over some of the underframe features, in particular the design of the radiator fan cowling, which was in danger of being so near the rails that it might contact the electrified third rail in the Bury area. This, it was agreed, was to be amended, as was the method of securing the engines, which was also deemed to be unsatisfactory. Sanding gear, which was planned for the batch, was also deleted at this stage, and Metro-Cammell was asked to look at the seat backs in the 1st Class section, which were deemed to be too tall. Subsequent to this visit the railcars' frame was redesigned and the engines were repositioned so that clearances for the battery boxes and radiator fans could be increased.

The Metro-Cammell cars are often referred to as 'Lightweights' by enthusiasts and historians, but were actually much heavier than the alloy Derby cars. The bodyframe was of steel sections, on to which were spot-welded steel side panels, while the ends of the vehicles were completely of steel, thus making them much stronger than the earlier Derby vehicles. Rolled steel sections were used for the underframe and these were fabricated together into a number of sub-structures, which included the headstocks. The only departure from the use of steel was on the roof, where the frame was made of aluminium alloy, covered with alloy sheeting. Vehicles were assembled using jigs similar to those that BR had used at Derby, and the bodies were insulated with sprayed asbestos. The bogies were of a fabricated design, which was similar to that used on the Derby cars, though of heavier construction in view of the increased weights involved.

Engines were the same AEC 150hp units as were being fitted to the Derby vehicles, while the gearboxes were again Wilson epicyclic. Wiring was carried out so as to be compatible with the 'Yellow Diamond' vehicles, and the controls were arranged in a similar fashion. Jumper cables

Right: The first of the Metro-Cammell units to be built is seen here on test at Sutton Park in late 1955 with DMBS M79076 leading. The front-end design was much criticised at the time, but attempts to get it modified came to nothing.
C. Banks Collection, Colour-Rail

were just below the cab windows and these early vehicles all had a valance below the buffer beam, through which the horns protruded.

The Bury-Bacup Metro-Cammells

The first to be completed, though not the first in numerical order, were the seven sets for the Bury area. Unlike in the Derby vehicles, no seats were provided after the second vestibule in the power car, which subsequently had a large guard's compartment and seated only 52 3rd Class passengers. The trailers had a 1st Class section, which again was different from any of the previous versions, seating 12 people in three rows, while providing seating for 53 in 2nd Class. The 3rd Class upholstery was maroon, while the 1st Class was in blue. By October 1955 the first set, 79076+79626, was out of the works and reported as being on test; in December 79082+79632 was sent to London for

inspection by officials. A press trip followed on 31 January 1956 from Manchester to Bury, after which Mr T. Polding, the District Passenger Manager, said he was anxious that the first experiment with diesels in Lancashire, with its increased service and cheap tickets, should be equally as successful as the schemes in the West Riding and Cumberland and he hoped this success might have some bearing on future developments.

Services commenced on 6 February 1956 with 35 trains a day being provided instead of the 16-19 of steam days, providing a 30-minute frequency for much of the day. Some services also continued through to Manchester Victoria via Heywood. Again passenger numbers increased dramatically, in the order of 135%, during the first few months following conversion, a rise that resulted in one of the new Derby Lightweights intended for the Manchester No 1 scheme to be brought in to provide additional capacity. Journey times from Bury to Bacup were reduced from 37 minutes to 34

minutes, which was little improvement on the steam service, and this caused an experiment to be carried out on one unit, which temporarily had its engines uprated to 165hp, but the modification was ultimately not adopted.

These seven sets, plus the Derby set, worked these services successfully until 1961, when 25 Cravens power-twin sets, specially fitted with 238hp engines, arrived.

Further routes were then dieselised, but then contraction of services following the Beeching Report allowed the original Metro-Cammell cars to be moved off to Buxton and Macclesfield, the transfer being complete by 1965; they were all withdrawn from there in July 1967 and cut up by T. W. Ward of Beighton in February 1968.

Right: Brand-new E79287 leads a Nottingham Victoria to Grantham service at Sedgebrook in multiple with a Derby Lightweight. The date is unknown but it may be the last day of passenger services at this station in 1956. *T. G. Hepburn, Rail Archive Stephenson*

The Bury-Bacup Metro-Cammells

Number	Type	Diagram	Lot No	Region	Set	Seats	Weight (tons)	Built	Partnered when new	Original depot
79076-79082	DMBS	592	30190	London Midland	Power-trailer	52	26t 10cwt	Dec 55	79626-79632	Bury
79626-79632	DTC	594	30191	London Midland	Power-trailer	12F/53S	25 tons	Dec 55	79076-79082	Bury

B.R. 592.

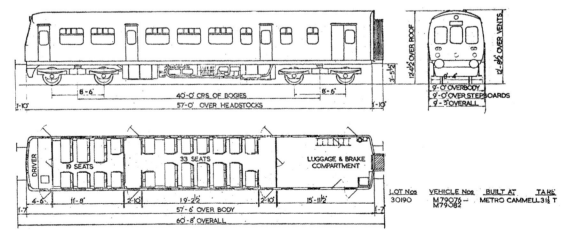

GANGWAYED MOTOR OPEN SECOND BRAKE

2-SECOND 52 SEATS
1-DRIVERS COMPARTMENT
1-LUGGAGE COMPARTMENT

Diagram 592

48

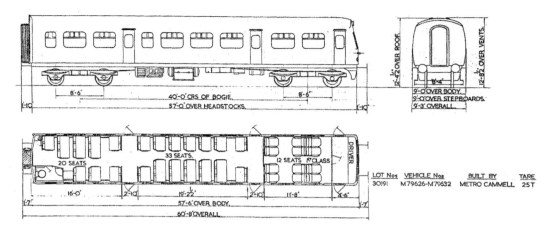

GANGWAYED DRIVING TRAILER OPEN COMPOSITE LAVATORY

I - FIRST 12 SEATS
2 - SECOND 53 SEATS
I - DRIVERS COMPARTMENT

Diagram 594

Above: One of the Metro-Cammell units originally allocated to Lincoln, E79062+E79278, passes Coke Ovens Junction on the approach to Lowestoft with the 10.00am service from Norwich on 22 May 1957. *K. L. Cook, Rail Archive Stephenson*

The East Anglia Metro-Cammells

With so many lightly used lines in the East of England it was natural that the area should be selected for further modernisation, and it was therefore decided that the bulk of the new two-car units ordered from Metro-Cammell should be sent there to allow for a further expansion of services. Twenty-nine two-car sets were provided and, though they were, in 1956, initially split between the Lincolnshire and East Anglia areas, all were in East Anglia by the following year. The Driving Motor Brakes were numbered E79047-E79075 and all seated 56. The external layout was similar to the Bury batch, but inside there was one row of forward-facing seats behind the rear vestibule, which made the guard's compartment slightly smaller. In a departure from other East Anglia sets and from the Bury Metro-Cammells, the Driving Trailers were built without a 1st Class compartment, and instead had a non-smoking 2nd Class section that seated 19, making the total capacity 72 people.

The first was completed in January 1956, with 79047+79263 and 79048+79264 arriving at Norwich on the 5th, having travelled under their own power from Birmingham. Enough of the rest were available to enable a substantial increase in diesel services to be introduced from the Summer timetable. Routes included were Thetford-Swaffham, Aldeburgh-Saxmundham-Ipswich, Harwich-Ipswich, Witham-Maldon, Witham-Braintree, Wickford-Southminster and St Mary's-Buntingford. Savings were estimated to be in the order of £72,000 per year.

Vehicles from this batch were used to work trains for the British Industries Fair in Castle Bromwich in April/May 1956, with 79061+79277, 79062+79278 and 79063+79279 being the three units involved, while two sets, 79055+79271 and 79056+79272, were sent to Scotland for three months, where they were used to test the suitability of a number of routes for diesel working. Deliveries were completed by August 1956. Interestingly, even before these were in service Metro-Cammell had received a huge order for 339 further vehicles, which were all to be of the 'Blue Square' arrangement and which would go on to become better known as Class 101.

Once the early transfers from Lincolnshire to East Anglia were complete, this batch remained at either Norwich or Stratford (and its sub-sheds) for their entire lives. They survived long enough for many to be painted in BR blue, but when much of the East Anglian railway system was butchered during the Beeching cuts they were left with no work and, due to their non-standard electrical arrangement, were early candidates for withdrawal. All were taken out of service in 1968 or 1969 and most were scrapped at Cohens of Kettering, Bird Group of Long Marston or T. W. Ward of Beighton. The exceptions were two power cars, E79047 and E79053, which entered departmental service as 975018 and 975019 and were used by the Railway Research Department at Derby for a number of projects, including linear rail vehicle propulsion tests and, as Lab 21, for plasma torch research. They were eventually scrapped in 1981.

Metro-Cammell cars

Number	Type	Diagram	Lot No	Region	Set	Seats	Weight	Built	Partnered with new	Original depot
79047-79056	DMBS	591	30190	Eastern	Power-trailer	56	26t 10cwt	Jan-Aug 56	79263-79272	Norwich
79057-79058									79273-79274	Stratford
79059-79064									79275-79280	Lincoln
79065-79066									79281-79282	Norwich
79067-79075									79283-79291	Lincoln

Number	Type	Diagram	Lot No	Region	Set	Seats	Weight	Built	Partnered with new	Original depot
79263-79272	DTS	593	30191	Eastern	Power-trailer	72	25 tons	Jan-Aug 56	79047-79056	Norwich
79273-79274									79057-79058	Stratford
79275-79280									79059-79064	Lincoln
79281-79282									79065-79066	Norwich
79283-79291									79067-79075	Lincoln

Left: Driving Motor Brake E79051 calls at Barton-on-Humber. The original three-line livery with the 'cycling lion' emblem can clearly be seen. *Colour-Rail*

BR 591

GANGWAYED MOTOR OPEN SECOND BRAKE

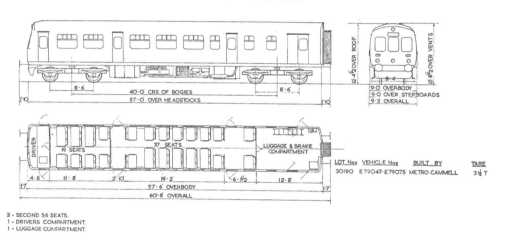

Diagram 591

LOT Nos	VEHICLE Nos	BUILT BY	TARE
30190	E79047-E79075	METRO CAMMELL	3½ T

2 - SECOND 56 SEATS.
1 - DRIVERS COMPARTMENT.
1 - LUGGAGE COMPARTMENT.

2 x 150 HP BUT ENGINES

BR 593

GANGWAYED DRIVING TRAILER OPEN SECOND LAVATORY

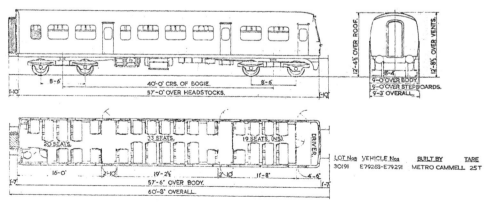

Diagram 593

LOT Nos	VEHICLE Nos	BUILT BY	TARE
30191	E79283-E79291	METRO CAMMELL	25T

3 - SECOND 72 SEATS
1 - DRIVER'S COMPARTMENT
1 - LAVATORY

NS - NON-SMOKING

Right: In East Anglia the Metro-Cammells became synonymous with the Norwich-Wells and Dereham-King's Lynn services. Norwich-based DTS E79270 leads a Dereham-bound train out of King's Lynn. *Colour-Rail*

Left: Together with other designs, the original batch of Metro-Cammells soon had the 'feather plume' or 'speed whiskers' painted on their ends, though the red buffer beams tended to become obscured by dirt. A unit is seen at the road crossing at Walsingham on its way to Wells. *Colour-Rail*

Right: Although the front windows on the Metro-Cammell sets were not as large as those on the Derby-built vehicles, they still offered a much better view than did locomotive-hauled stock. As a result they were very popular for rail tours, such as this one on 10 October 1960, when a six-car set visited Edgware GNR station, at that time still in use as a goods depot, but subsequently closed in 1964. The single line from Camden Town was originally intended to extend further to serve housing, which in the event was never developed. *Colour-Rail*

Left: Unlike the later Metro-Cammell-built Class 101s, the early units had a fairing below the buffer beam, through which the horns protruded. This example is seen at Melton Constable on 20 March 1962. *Colour-Rail*

Right: Many of the East Anglia-allocated Metro-Cammells were repainted with only two bodyside stripes during their lifetime so that they could be paired with the Derby vehicles, either in sets or in multiple. One set so treated is seen at Saxmundham on 24 September 1964. *Colour-Rail*

Left: There were many individual variations in colour schemes, and later some of the Metro-Cammells had their buffer beam skirts painted red to match the buffer beams. Many also received the yellow warning panel. *Colour-Rail*

Top: In the final years of their lives many of the Metro-Cammells were painted in BR blue with full yellow ends, resulting in a rather bland appearance. Jumper cables were also permanently fitted to most sets.
J. J. Davis, Colour-Rail

Middle: Arriving at its final destination of Ipswich on 6 April 1963 is Metro-Cammell power car E79054, which has received the two-stripe livery and has the protective pads fitted behind the driver's cabs to prevent body damage from tokens.
Alec Swain,
www.transporttreasury.co.uk

Below: Most of the Metro-Cammells spent their lives working lines in remote areas with little traffic, so it is no wonder that they were all made surplus by the Beeching cuts. A Lowestoft-Ipswich service is seen near Darsham on the East Suffolk Line on 31 March 1964.
J. F. Oxley

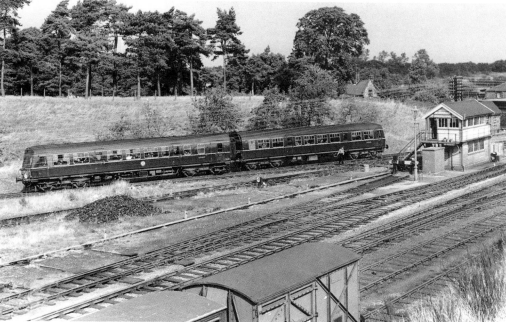

Above: Parcels and sundries traffic was always heavy in East Anglia, and the Metro-Cammell brake compartments were always regarded as too small. A unit accelerates away from Wroxham during September 1966 while a porter carries off the boxes it has just left. *Colour-Rail*

Middle: Relief signalman S. Howard at Wymondham box has just taken the token from the driver of the 11.36am King's Lynn to Norwich service; it is being worked by E79067+E79274, which are not an original pairing but were both in the two-stripe livery by the time of this photograph, taken on 9 September 1967. *G. R. Mortimer*

Bottom: In this wonderful period piece a Metro-Cammell unit is seen in the bay at Wells-next-the-Sea station while a railwayman, complete with bike clips and flat hat, ambles down the platform to his work. *David Lawrence*

9

The North Eastern (Newcastle) sets

It was not surprising that the North Eastern Region was to feature so prominently in the introduction of the new lightweight diesel trains, as the Region and its predecessors had been searching for economical replacement traction for steam locomotives and stock for many years.

The North Eastern area of the former LNER had introduced one of the first internal combustion railcars, in 1903, with its petrol-electric No 3170, and had possessed a large number of steam-powered Sentinel railcars, which operated round the Scarborough and Whitby areas from the 1920s; some had lasted until 1949. There had also been four experimental Armstrong-Whitworth cars and one Metro-Cammell/Ganz, just before the Second World War.

After the war the LNER had wanted to buy 59 diesel railcars and had even borrowed two of the GWR examples, Nos 6 and 19, during 1944, and these had been trialled in Tyneside, as well as around Harrogate. Following nationalisation there were more trials, this time with GWR No 20, which worked Leeds-Harrogate and Wakefield-Doncaster services for a time.

The 1952 report had listed services between Newcastle and Carlisle as suitable candidates for the early introduction of lightweight diesel trains, and these were high in the list of priorities in a scheme that was ranked only third behind that of the West Riding and Lincolnshire. The 60-mile route took in areas with a population of 600,000, most of

Above: One of the four-car Newcastle sets is seen arriving at Redcar on 11 June 1962. The Driving Motor Second, which had a conventional window layout, is leading. These cars were not fitted with a toilet and therefore had clear glass in the rear window at this side. *Colour-Rail*

whom lived in either Carlisle or Tyneside, with the area between Hexham and Carlisle being sparsely populated. The steam service consisted of 12 up and 11 down trains a day, but it was envisaged that traffic could increase by 20% if a more frequent service was to be provided. Ten four-car units were proposed at a cost of £500,000, which it was hoped would save the railway around £44,000 per year in costs, while providing an improved service. The ten units would replace 18 steam engines and 40 coaches and would enable Hexham locomotive depot to be closed.

In the event the order was cut back to just five four-car units and the scheme was altered so that it encompassed services operating between Newcastle and Middlesbrough, which included the heavy traffic carried between Tyneside, Wearside and Teesside. During October 1954 one of the almost-new Leeds-Bradford sets, E79007+E79507, travelled north for tests and was used on trial runs between Newcastle, Middlesbrough and Saltburn.

Unlike previous Derby sets these trains were to be permanently made up of four cars, comprising a Driving Motor Composite, a Trailer Second, a Trailer Brake Second and a Driving Motor Second. There were a considerable number of differences from earlier batches of vehicles, including the provision of 2+2 seating in all 2nd Class areas, instead of the 2+3 used on previous batches. The Driving Motor Composite at one end of the train was built to a unique configuration that saw 12 1st Class seats in the usual location but also a further eight in a 1st Class non-smoking compartment to the rear of the first vestibule. So that these would line up with the windows, only three large panes were provided in the centre section, with a gap between the first and the second, instead of the three large and one small of the normal driving vehicles. Unusually for a 1st Class vehicle, no lavatory was provided. The Driving Motor Second at the other end of the set was to the normal body layout, except that the toilet compartment, which would normally have been fitted to a vehicle of this design, was omitted. In between were two trailer vehicles, without driving cabs; both were fitted with a toilet, and one with a guard's compartment. A total of 206 2nd Class seats were provided. These five pairs of centre cars were the only ones built to the original Derby Lightweight design, but the idea was repeated later in similar vehicles of other classes ordered from Derby Works and Metro-Cammell.

As had by now become standard, the sets were equipped with AEC 150hp engines, two under each of the outer cars, and the gearboxes were the Wilson type. Controls and coupling systems were compatible with all the other vehicles except for the West Riding sets. All five sets were received by South Gosforth Depot in September 1955 and each was tested on the closed-to-passengers Ponteland branch, where driver training also took place. Introduction to service was on Monday 21 November, once staff training had been completed, and the new units replaced seven of the existing steam-hauled services each way per hour with accelerations

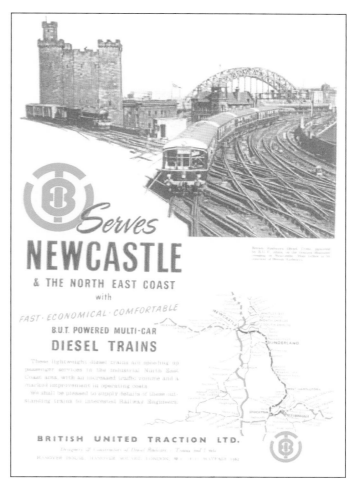

of between 12 and 22 minutes for each journey. Some trains at peak times were formed of more than one set, and a trolley service was also introduced on some trains. As with the earlier schemes passenger numbers climbed remarkably

Left: The north east four-car sets had a unique layout in one of the driving vehicles, as the 1st Class area extended into the centre saloon. This meant that there were fewer windows so that they lined up with the seats, as can be seen on E79508. Also unique were the non-driving Trailer Brakes used with this batch. *British Railways*

Above: The driving cars at the other end of the north east four-car sets were also unique in that they had 2nd Class seating throughout, but no brake compartment or lavatory. E79153 is seen in this official photograph, dated November 1955. *British Railways*

Below: The north east four-car units were extensively tested before being brought into service and one is seen here near Darlington South Junction in November 1955, attracting much interest from permanent way workers. *J. W. Armstrong*

and four two-car Derby Lightweights were added in March 1956, which enabled trains to be made up of four, six or eight coaches as required. These did not repeat the internal layout of the previous four-car sets; the Driving Motor Brake Seconds were equipped with a brake compartment while the Driving Trailer had the 1st Class section in the usual place, behind the driver, and also had a toilet fitted in the standard position by the gangway. Seating was to the 3+2 pattern, which meant that 52 people could be seated in the DMBS, and 53 2nd Class and 16 1st Class in the DMC. The DMBS vehicles had a guard's compartment that occupied the whole area between the rear vestibule and the rear of the coach, the first time that this layout had been used on a Derby car, these alterations making no difference to the external appearance.

Driving vehicles were equipped with four marker lights with no provision for a red light to be shown, other than by using a shade (although the use of a tail lamp was more common).

Dieselisation of the North Eastern Region proceeded much more quickly than in other areas, largely due to the enthusiasm of Mr Frank Hick, Assistant to the Chief Regional Officer (General), and as a result many production types of units flowed into the area enabling diesel services to be extended. By February 1957 there were sufficient new units to enable the Newcastle-Carlisle line to be modernised, as envisaged in the original 1952 plan. Although the bulk of services were worked by four-car Metro-Cammell units, the two-car Derby Lightweights were often used to supplement services on this line.

Most Newcastle-Sunderland trains went over to the diesels in September 1957, and a rejig of duties caused the Derby Lightweights to be reallocated to closed diagrams such as Newcastle to Carlisle, where they would not be required to work into other areas or work with units that had an incompatible coupling code.

The North Eastern Region received an avalanche of new DMUs up to 1960 and was quick to turn over all its minor lines to multiple unit operation. Although traffic was increased by the new trains, many of the smaller lines were still uneconomic and many were closed during the 1960s, leading to the Region having a substantial surplus of rolling stock.

By the mid-1960s the earliest Derby Lightweights were suffering from some problems and, due to their non-standard coupling systems, became candidates for withdrawal, despite being only around ten years old. All the four-car units were taken out of service in 1966 and 1967, with a few cars enjoying a temporary reprieve at Leith before withdrawal. Most were scrapped around 1971, with cutting taking place at various locations, including South Gosforth, Heaton TMD, Darlington C&W and at contractors such as T. W. Ward and T. J. Thomson.

Three of the two-car units, 79137/38/40 with trailers 79658/60/61, were transferred to Cambridge (which was a stronghold of the 'Yellow Diamond' cars) around 1966, while the fourth, 79139+79659, had been scrapped in 1963. It should be noted that by the time of the first scrapping the sets do not appear to have been running with their original trailers. These remaining sets hung on until June 1968 when they too were withdrawn and scrapped by contractors in East Anglia.

Newcastle area sets

Four-car sets

Number	Type	Diagram	Lot No	Set	Seats	Built	Partnered when new	Original depot	Withdrawn
79150-79154	DMS	518	30193	Four-car	64	Sept 55	79325-79329 79400-79404 79508-79512	South Gosforth	1966-67
79325-79329	TBSL	508	30194	Four-car	45	Sept 55	79150-79154 79400-79404 79508-79512	South Gosforth	1966-67
79400-79404	TSL	517	30195	Four-car	61	Sept 55	79508-79512 79325-79329 79150-79154	South Gosforth	1966-67
79508-79512	DMC	502	30192	Four-car	20F/36S	Sept 55	79325-79329 79400-79404 79150-79154	South Gosforth	1966-67

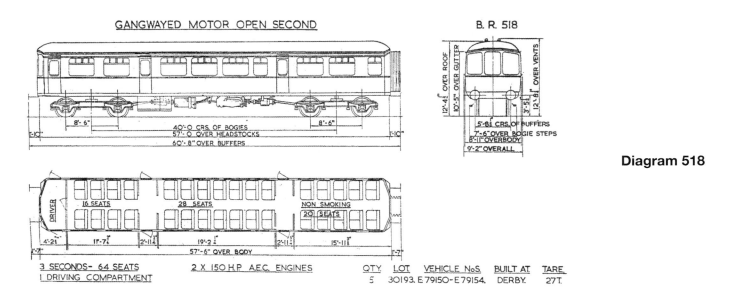

Diagram 518

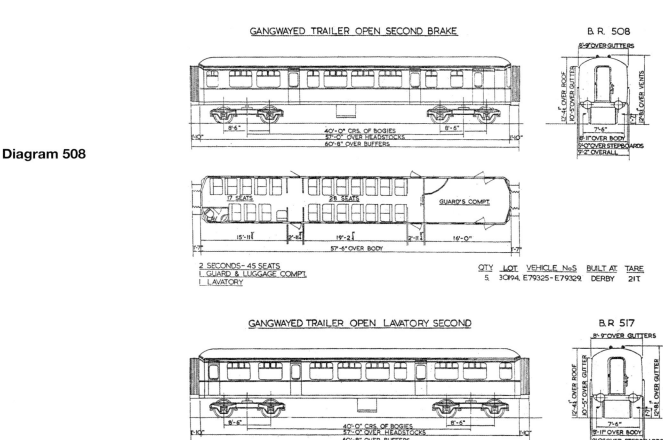

Diagram 508

GANGWAYED TRAILER OPEN SECOND BRAKE

B.R. 508

17 SEATS 28 SEATS GUARD'S COMPT.

2 SECONDS – 45 SEATS
1 GUARD & LUGGAGE COMPT.
1 LAVATORY

QTY	LOT	VEHICLE NoS.	BUILT AT	TARE
5	30194	E79325 - E79329	DERBY	21T

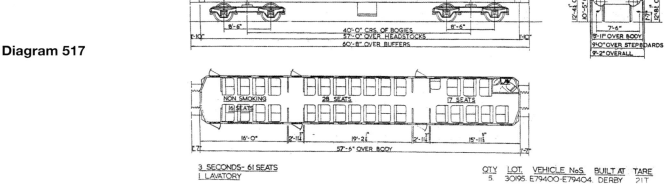

Diagram 517

GANGWAYED TRAILER OPEN LAVATORY SECOND

B.R. 517

NON SMOKING 16 SEATS 28 SEATS 17 SEATS

3 SECONDS – 61 SEATS
1 LAVATORY

QTY	LOT	VEHICLE NoS.	BUILT AT	TARE
5	30195	E79400 - E79404	DERBY	21T

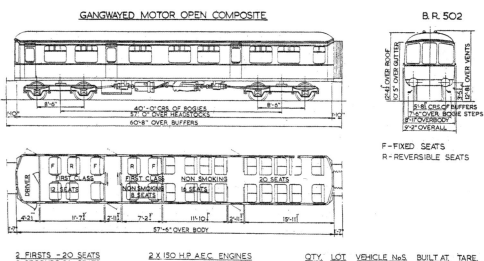

Diagram 502

GANGWAYED MOTOR OPEN COMPOSITE

B.R. 502

F – FIXED SEATS
R – REVERSIBLE SEATS

DRIVER FIRST CLASS 12 SEATS FIRST CLASS NON SMOKING 8 SEATS NON SMOKING 16 SEATS 20 SEATS

2 FIRSTS – 20 SEATS
2 SECONDS – 36 SEATS
1 DRIVING COMPARTMENT

2 X 150 H.P. A.E.C. ENGINES

QTY	LOT	VEHICLE NoS.	BUILT AT	TARE
5	30192	E79508 - E79512	DERBY	27T

Left: Some of the services required the sets to be doubled up, and this was the case on 16 February 1957 for this Middlesbrough-Newcastle working. *J. S. Phillips*

Right: On 5 July 1959, with DMS E79151 leading, one of the four-car sets passes Billingham. *Ian Allan Library*

Left: With DMS E79150 leading, one of the north east four-car sets is seen on a Blyth working at Monkseaton. *P. J. Sharpe*

Right: Two of the four-car north east sets are seen bound for Middlesbrough, with one of the "Driving Motor Composites leading. These were the only cars with this window arrangement. *T. G. Hepburn, Rail Archive Stephenson*

Two-car sets

Number	Type	Diagram	Lot No	Set	Seats	Built	Partnered when new	Original depot	Withdrawn
79137-79140	DMBS	527	30240	Power-trailer	52	Mar 56	79658-79661	South Gosforth	1963-68
79658-79661	DTCL	631	30241	Power-trailer	16F/53S	Mar 56	79137-79140	South Gosforth	1963-68

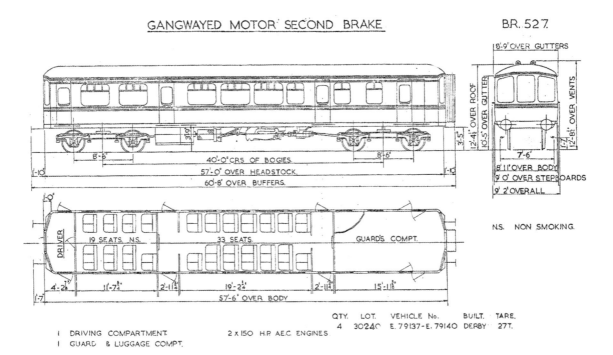

GANGWAYED MOTOR SECOND BRAKE   BR. 527.

8'-9" OVER GUTTERS

12'-4¼" OVER ROOF
10'-5" OVER GUTTER
12'-8½" OVER VENTS

7'-6"

8'-11" OVER BODY
9'-0" OVER STEPBOARDS
9'-2" OVERALL

3'-9"   3'-5"

8'-6"   40'-0" CRS OF BOGIES   8'-6"
1'-10   57'-0" OVER HEADSTOCK   1'-10
60'-8" OVER BUFFERS.

N.S.   NON SMOKING.

1'-0"
DRIVER   19 SEATS. N.S.   33 SEATS.   GUARD'S COMPT.

4'-2⅞"   11'-7¾"   2'-11¼"   19'-2¼"   2'-11¼"   15'-1⅛"
1'-7   57'-6" OVER BODY

QTY.	LOT.	VEHICLE No.	BUILT.	TARE.
4	30240	E. 79137-E. 79140	DERBY	27T.

1 DRIVING COMPARTMENT.
1 GUARD & LUGGAGE COMPT.

2 x 150 H.P. A.E.C. ENGINES

Diagram 527

Above: Four two-car sets were allocated to the Newcastle area for strengthening purposes, and the first of these, with DMBS E79137 leading and another set in the rear, leaves Darlington station on 27 July 1963 heading south. The yellow warning panel has been crudely painted over the 'speed whiskers'. These sets eventually gravitated to Cambridge. *Colour-Rail*

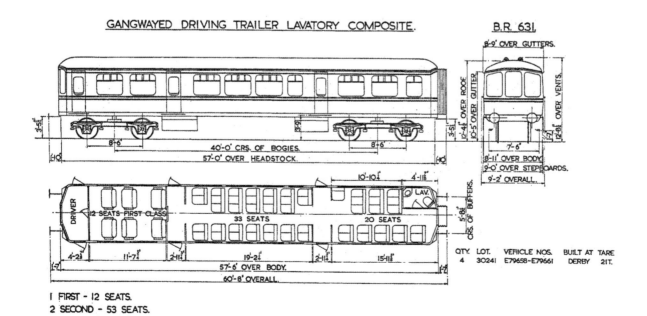

GANGWAYED DRIVING TRAILER LAVATORY COMPOSITE.   B.R. 631.

QTY.	LOT.	VEHICLE NOS.	BUILT AT	TARE
4	30241	E79658-E79661	DERBY	21T.

1 FIRST - 12 SEATS.
2 SECOND - 53 SEATS.
1 DRIVING COMPARTMENT.
1 LAVATORY.

Diagram 631

10

Birmingham area Lightweights

One of the first urban areas to receive the diesel treatment was that surrounding Birmingham. There, as in Yorkshire, the trains were under heavy competition from buses and were seen by the public as outdated and dirty.

A limited scheme was first approved by the British Transport Commission in February 1955, and to raise public interest in diesels three two-car units, which were in fact the first three Derby Lightweights completed for the East Anglia scheme, were used to bring passengers to the British Industries Fair at Castle Bromwich, which opened on 2 May 1955. The loan period lasted from 18 April to 13 May, and the new units were well received by visitors.

The original scheme would have seen 15 sets, of mixed power-twin and power-trailer types, introduced. These sets were to be based at Monument Lane Carriage Sidings, in the Ladywood area of the city and about half a mile from the existing steam engine shed.

Members of the Light Weight Trains Committee visited the site that April to see how work was progressing on the depot, and noted that pits were being deepened and a new access road made. Storage tanks for diesel fuel and oil had to be built on the site and this necessitated additional adjacent land being purchased in this heavily crowded area. The cost of providing the conversions to the depot was £18,800.

Above: Working a Birmingham via Aston service, this Derby Lightweight is seen at Four Oaks on 11 March 1956. Savings in crew costs are already evident. *E. S. Russell, Colour-Rail*

According to the London Midland Region's official records, a revised scheme was then devised, which would have seen nine two-car sets and four three-car sets provided – presumably the three-car sets being used in place of two two-car sets at rush hours and enabling a reduction in the total number of sets required. However, before this plan was able to come to fruition delays in the implementation of the Manchester scheme allowed the transfer of 13 sets from that allocation, meaning that Birmingham ended up with 26 sets, all of which were of two cars.

The Birmingham Lightweights were constructed immediately after the last of the East Anglia sets, though there was a slight delay of a couple of months between the two, with 79118 and its partner 79639 not appearing until November 1955. As they were not immediately required in Birmingham, the first three were sent on short-term loan to Carlisle, but were back in time for the start of services.

All of the DMBSs were of the large-guard's-compartment type, similar to those delivered to Newcastle, and seated 52, but there were some differences in the trailers, with three different design codes being used. Those built to diagram 509 had three rows of 2+1 1st Class seats, providing accommodation for nine people; those to code 511 had four rows of 2+1 seats; and those to code 642 has three rows of 2+2 seating, both the latter designs having accommodation for 12 people.

It was during the construction of this batch of units that the idea of some form of decoration on the cab front was first discussed. In November 1955 one recently completed unit intended for Birmingham was painted with yellow diagonal lines on one end and red and white on the other, but railway officials felt that this spoiled the overall appearance. One set had already been given a red buffer beam, and this was said to be 'beneficial'. By December it had been decided that the ends of the units should receive what was then called a 'feather plume' in cream, although this design soon gained the universal name of the 'speed whisker' and was applied throughout the whole DMU fleet over the following few years.

Services between Birmingham New Street, Sutton Coldfield and Lichfield began on 5 March 1956, with other routes being added as deliveries allowed. The last unit was delivered by May 1956.

Traffic in the Birmingham area rose rapidly after the introduction of the diesel units and in the end a special batch of three-car suburban units, later Class 117, was built to work trains there. As in other areas, it was soon found that the Derby Lightweights' inability to work in multiple with later stock was an operational issue that caused much inconvenience, and as a result attempts were made to group the Lightweight cars into areas where they would only have to couple up to each other.

The first three were back in Carlisle by 1959, while others went to Llandudno Junction and the Liverpool area. Most of them then settled at Macclesfield for some years but, when that went 'Blue Square', more moved to Carlisle and Cambridge. Ultimately there were too many diesel units to work the services that British Railways had left, and the Lightweights were withdrawn en masse between 1967 and 1969.

Left: Less than a week after the start of railcar services in the Birmingham area, on 10 March 1956, two of the new units are seen at Four Oaks station, providing a complete contrast to the dingy steam-hauled stock stored in the background. *E. S. Russell, Colour-Rail*

Left: It was the practice in the early years to use to use the upper marker light to show that a train was working a stopping passenger service, thus replicating the codes used by steam locomotives. A number of the Derby Lightweights are seen in multiple at Lichfield City on 11 August 1957. *E. S. Russell, Colour-Rail*

Derby Lightweight cars originally allocated to the Birmingham area

Number	Type	Diagram	Lot No	Region	Set	Seats	Weight	Built	Partnered when new	Original depot
79118-79126	DMBS	633	30235	London Midland	Power-trailer	52	27 tons	Nov 55-Jan 56	79639-79647	Monument Lane
79127-79134	DMBS	633	30240	London Midland	Power-trailer	52	27 tons	Feb-Mar 56	79648-79655	Monument Lane
79141	DMBS	633	30246	London Midland	Power-trailer	52	27 tons	Apr-July 56	79662	Monument Lane
79143-79149	DMBS	633	30201	London Midland	Power-trailer	52	27 tons	Jan-Feb 56	79663-79669	Monument Lane
79169-79170	DMBS	633	30321	London Midland	Power-trailer	52	27 tons	Apr-July 56	79670-79671	Monument Lane
79639-79647	DTCL	509	30236	London Midland	Power-trailer	9F/53S	21 tons	Nov 55-Jan 56	79118-79126	Monument Lane
79648-79655	DTCL	509	30241	London Midland	Power-trailer	9F/53S	21 tons	Feb-Mar 56	79127-79134	Monument Lane
79662	DTCL	642	30247	London Midland	Power-trailer	12F/53S	21 tons	Apr 56	79141	Monument Lane
79663-79669	DTCL	642	30202	London Midland	Power-trailer	12F/53S	21 tons	Jan-Feb 56	79143-79149	Monument Lane
79670-79671	DTCL	511	30322	London Midland	Power-trailer	12F/53S	21 tons	Apr-May 56	79169-79170	Monument Lane

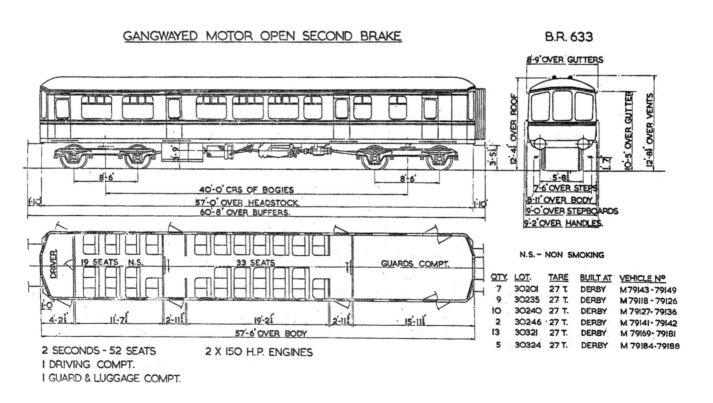

GANGWAYED MOTOR OPEN SECOND BRAKE   B.R. 633

8-9' OVER GUTTERS

12-4' OVER ROOF

10-5' OVER GUTTER

12-8' OVER VENTS

3-9

8-6'   8-6'

40'-0' CRS OF BOGIES

57'-0' OVER HEADSTOCK.

60'-8' OVER BUFFERS.

5-8'

7-6' OVER STEPS

8-11' OVER BODY

9-0' OVER STEPBOARDS

9-2' OVER HANDLES.

DRIVER   19 SEATS N.S.   33 SEATS   GUARDS COMPT.

4-2½'   11'-7½'   2'-11½'   19'-2½'   2'-11½'   15'-11½'

57'-6' OVER BODY

N.S. - NON SMOKING

QTY.	LOT.	TARE	BUILT AT	VEHICLE Nº
7	30201	27 T.	DERBY	M 79143-79149
9	30235	27 T.	DERBY	M 79118-79126
10	30240	27 T.	DERBY	M 79127-79136
2	30246	27 T.	DERBY	M 79141-79142
13	30321	27 T.	DERBY	M 79169-79181
5	30324	27 T.	DERBY	M 79184-79188

2 SECONDS - 52 SEATS   2 X 150 H.P. ENGINES

1 DRIVING COMPT.

1 GUARD & LUGGAGE COMPT.

Diagram 633

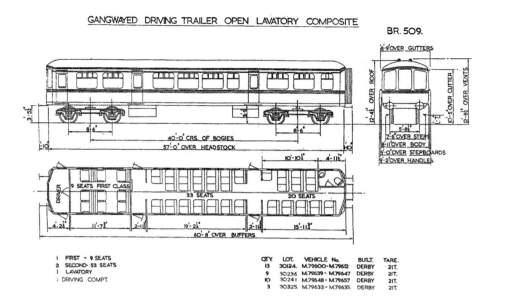

GANGWAYED DRIVING TRAILER OPEN LAVATORY COMPOSITE

BR. 509.

Diagram 509

1 FIRST - 9 SEATS
2 SECOND - 53 SEATS
1 LAVATORY
1 DRIVING COMPT.

QTY.	LOT.	VEHICLE No.	BUILT.	TARE.
13	30124.	M.79600-M.79612	DERBY	21T.
9	30236	M.79639 - M.79647	DERBY	21T.
10	30241	M.79648 - M.79657	DERBY	21T.
3	30325.	M.79633 - M.79635.	DERBY	21T.

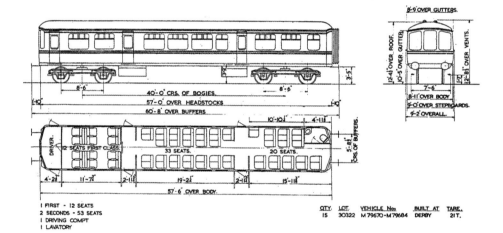

GANGWAYED DRIVING TRAILER LAVATORY COMPOSITE

B.R. 511.

Diagram 511

1 FIRST - 12 SEATS
2 SECONDS - 53 SEATS
1 DRIVING COMPT
1 LAVATORY

QTY.	LOT.	VEHICLE Nos	BUILT AT	TARE.
15	30322	M 79670-M 79684	DERBY	21T.

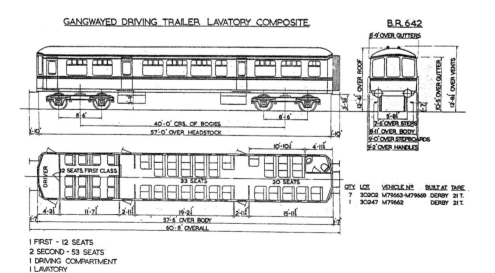

GANGWAYED DRIVING TRAILER LAVATORY COMPOSITE

B.R. 642

Diagram 642

QTY	LOT	VEHICLE Nº	BUILT AT	TARE
7	30202	M79663-M79669	DERBY	21 T.
1	30247	M79662	DERBY	21 T.

1 FIRST - 12 SEATS
2 SECOND - 53 SEATS
1 DRIVING COMPARTMENT
1 LAVATORY

Right: Wherever the new trains went they created massive interest. Enthusiasts of all ages are anxious to capture all the details of the first Lightweight DMU to reach the Cardiff area on Sunday 18 November 1956. It is working an excursion from Coventry and Birmingham New Street to Cardiff. *P. Sampson*

Left: The new DMUs were extremely popular for excursions. Four of the Birmingham-based sets are pictured at Bath while heading an excursion for Bournemouth, presumably via the Somerset & Dorset line. *R. E. Toop*

Right: The 1.36pm Lichfield City to Birmingham New Street service arrives at Aston on 14 December 1957, with Driving Trailer M79644 leading. *M. Mensing*

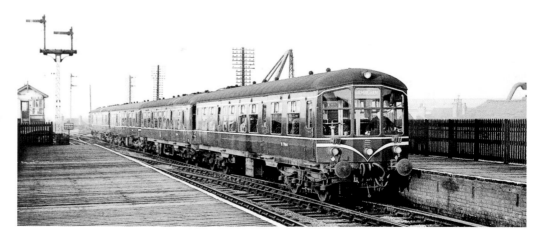

Left: Most of the Birmingham area duties involved multiple working of units. Driving Trailer M79654 leads into Sutton Coldfield, showing that these sets were very soon adorned with the 'feather plume', much later to be universally known as 'speed whiskers'. *P. J. Sharpe*

Below: Sutton Coldfield station was one of those that saw heavy railcar traffic, as can be seen on 26 May 1958 with two heavily loaded trains present. *P. J. Sharpe*

Left: M79654 was one of the original batch allocated to Monument Lane, but soon moved on to Llandudno Junction, where it was a staple of North Wales services for some years. It is seen here at Birmingham New Street while working a Wolverhampton to Coventry service on 29 September 1956. *Ian Allan Library*

11

The North Wales sets

The idea of using some of the new railcars in North Wales seems to have first been suggested in September 1953 when A. E. Hammett, Commercial Superintendent at Euston, suggested that lightweight diesel trains might be the answer to a problem the London Midland Region had with the branch line from Llandudno Junction to Blaenau Ffestiniog. Although this line carried substantial summer traffic, for much of the rest of the year it ran at a considerable loss due to the sparsely populated area through which it ran. Consideration had been given to closure, but the roads in the surrounding areas were very poor and were unsuitable for use by a replacement bus service.

This observation came more than a year after the publication of the Light Weight Trains Committee's original report, by which time the Committee was eagerly seeking other lines that would benefit from the introduction of modern traction. However, approval for any scheme for North Wales seems to have taken a low priority, for it was November the following year before the Committee was told that the BTC was likely to imminently approve funding. Even then it was to be February 1955 before a scheme was finally agreed to provide six sets, a number that was upgraded by one four months later.

On 25 and 26 July officers went on one of their inspection tours, which usually preceded dieselisation, travelling from Euston by special saloon and visiting the

Above: One of the North Wales-allocated sets, possibly on an Amlwch working, is pictured in the bay platform at Bangor during the 1959 Easter holidays. *J. H. Moss, Colour-Rail*

Blaenau branch, the Amlwch branch on Anglesey and the Rhyl-Denbigh line, the result of which was a decision to use the new trains on both the Bangor-Amlwch services and the Llandudno-Blaenau line.

Although seven sets were officially allocated, the area initially received 13 as, for reasons that will be explained in the next chapter, some of those ordered for the Manchester No 1 scheme were not yet required there. The allocation also included a spare trailer, 79683, which was later to find its way to Manchester. The origins of this are a bit of a mystery, as it does not appear in official records as a separate order. It is possible that it was to be the trailer for 79182, which was never completed as originally intended but which was taken from the Manchester order and finished as a double-ended power car and given the number 79900. Certainly the sequence of numbers would bear this out.

Although the sets allocated to North Wales were from different lot numbers, they were all built to the same pattern and had the large guard's compartment, similar to the Birmingham vehicles, with 52 3rd Class seats in the

Driving Motor Brake. The trailers were again to two different specifications, some having nine and some 12 1st Class seats, in a similar way to the Birmingham order.

Within a short space of time some of those sets originally allocated were sent back to Manchester, with initially Llandudno retaining only 79135/36 and 79173/75/81, together with their respective partners. However, before long some of the Birmingham-allocated units (79126-34) together with their trailers were transferred to Wales, although the area then lost 79173/75/81, meaning that the allocation settled to 79126-36. It also later gained, at various times and from Manchester, a batch of five Driving Motor Brakes, 79184-88, which were paired with Driving Motor Composites 79189-93. These being non-standard, 79191-93 were converted to Driving Trailers 79633-79635, while 79189/90 stayed in their original form. More details of these conversions are given in the next chapter.

Services to Blaenau Ffestiniog began on 5 March 1956, and those to Amlwch commenced on 28 May. A maintenance depot was located at Llandudno Junction, and £4,000 was spent on upgrading it for its new use.

Although the North Wales services were very successful, the Bangor-Amlwch service was closed under the Beeching axe in 1964, leaving the area with some excess capacity. The Derby Lightweights were gradually transferred away to other destinations such as Bletchley and Macclesfield and more modern 'Blue Square' vehicles arrived to work the Blaenau branch and other services. By 1966 there were no Lightweights working from Llandudno Junction. All those allocated to the North Wales scheme were scrapped as non-standard between 1967 and 1969, mostly by local scrap merchants in the areas to which they were last allocated.

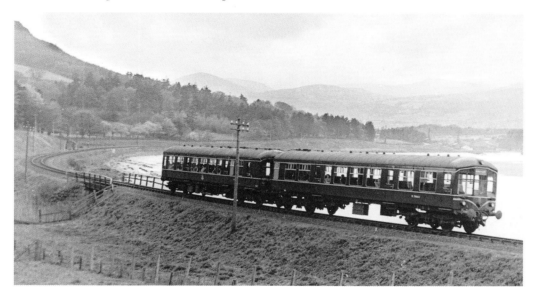

Left: The diesels proved to be a huge success in North Wales, partly due to the scenery. Power trailer set M79172 and M79673 are pictured near Tal-y-Cafn heading for Blaenau Ffestiniog in May 1956. *H. Rodgers Jones*

Left: In 1957 one of the Llandudno Junction power cars, M79135, was experimentally fitted with automatic gear-changing equipment and is seen here calling at Betws-y-Coed during the time it was so equipped. The car later reverted to normal configuration. *Ian Allan Library*

Original allocation of Derby Lightweights to North Wales

Number	Type	Diagram	Lot No	Region	Set	Seats	Weight	Built	Partnered when new	Original depot
79135-79136	DMBS	633	30240	London Midland	Power-trailer	52	27 tons	Feb-Mar 56	79656-79657	Llandudno Junction
79171-79181	DMBS	633	30321	London Midland	Power-trailer	52	27 tons	Apr-July 56	79672-79682	Llandudno Junction
79656-79657	DTCL	509	30241	London Midland	Power-trailer	9F/53S	21 tons	Feb-Mar 56	79135-79136	Llandudno Junction
79672-79682, 79683	DTCL	511	30322	London Midland	Power-trailer	12F/53S	21 tons	Apr-May 56	79171-79181	Spare Llandudno

Diagrams for this table are on pages 66/67

Right: Five power-twins were transferred to Wales from Manchester, of which three were later converted to power-trailers. One of the two Driving Motor Composites that retained their engines was M79190, seen here leaving Conway with the 3.15pm Bangor to Llandudno Junction service on 6 September 1957. *K. L. Cook, Rail Archive Stephenson*

Right: The Amlwch branch was the first service in North Wales to be turned over to DMUs. On 30 April 1964, not long before the branch closed, a unit is seen waiting to return to Bangor. *Colour-Rail*

Left: Five power twins, which had been originally ordered for the Manchester No 1 scheme, were also used in North Wales from 1962. One of them works a Llandudno-bound service in the mid-1960s, by which time it has received the half-yellow front end. *D. A. Hope, Colour-Rail*

Below: In May 1959 a four-car unit heads through Pont-y-Pant with a Blaenau Ffestiniog-bound service. *Colour-Rail*

Above: One of the sets transferred from Birmingham to Wales around 1959 was M79133 and trailer M79654, and they stayed in the area until around 1966. The set is seen at the old Blaenau Ffestiniog North station. *Ian Allan Library*

Below: Among the scenic delights of North Wales were the town walls at Conway. One of the North Wales units passes under the walls while working from Llandudno Junction to Bangor. *Kenneth Field, Rail Archive Stephenson*

12

The Manchester area sets

Unlike the earlier schemes, which were cut and dried and which covered a specific area, those subsequently planned for the big cities are much more difficult to keep track of.

The first sign that dieselisation was planned for Manchester was when tests were carried out between Stockport, Buxton and Miller's Dale in early January 1955. Three recently built vehicles intended for the West Cumberland scheme were involved – Driving Motor Brakes 79017 and 79019 and Driving Trailer 79609 – which were used in three-car form. The units travelled to Longsight direct from Derby Works to take part in timing trials to test the practicality of operating railcars over the steeply graded Buxton lines. With a current time for steam traction for the route of 49 minutes uphill, it was hoped that the railcars could manage 40 minutes, but in the event they completed the course in 35, with speed never falling below 40mph on the steepest grade, which was 1 in 58. The tests were judged to be an outstanding success.

The Manchester No 1 scheme was originally allocated 25 two-car sets with the intention of converting services to Buxton and on the Styal route, but some members of the London Midland Region management preferred that the modernisation of the Styal line was to be left until the promised electrification came about, and that converting to diesels in the interim was unnecessary.

Above: 'Under the wires' and heading for Macclesfield, this power-trailer is exhibiting one marker light above the cab as a sign that it is working a stopping passenger train. It is about to pick up passengers at Guide Bridge. *Colour-Rail*

As a result, when a request was received in June 1955 for some of Manchester's as yet undelivered Derby Lightweights to be reallocated to the Birmingham No 1 scheme, this was agreed. Other sets were to be lent to Llandudno Junction and one was to go to Bury to strengthen the successful Metro-Cammell sets operating there. Official records show that two power cars were also transferred to the Banbury-Bletchley scheme; presumably these had been intended to be 79182 and 79183, whose numbers fall within the Manchester batch, but which were never built, and which probably eventually surfaced as the two single cars 79900 and 79901.

Longsight Depot therefore only received three sets from new, these being power-twins DMBSs 79186-8 and DMCs 79191-3, but these were soon bolstered by power-trailer sets DMBS 79171/72/74/76-80 with DTC trailers 79672/73/75/77-81 and power-twins DMBS 79184-85 and DMCs 79189-90, which had been at Llandudno Junction, giving 13 sets in total. Driving Motor Brake 79142 and trailer 79684 were separately allocated to Bury to work alongside the new Metro-Cammell vehicles there.

The power-twins – doubtless originally ordered for the hilly Buxton route – followed the by now standard large-guard's-compartment design, seating 52, while the Driving Motor Composites with which they were paired had 1st Class accommodation for nine people. The power-trailers had the same design of DMBS vehicles but the Driving Trailers had 1st Class seating for 12 people.

Once all the politics had been sorted out, which took some time, services began between Manchester (London Road) and Buxton on 8 October 1956, with the short branch to Miller's Dale being added on the 14th, as were services to Macclesfield. Other services around the city were gradually added as time went on and the complete scheme was not in operation until February 1958, by which time railcars from Metro-Cammell, Gloucester, Park Royal and Birmingham Railway Carriage & Wagon Works had been added to the fleet.

The influx of new units caused the Derby Lightweights to become non-standard as they were incapable of being coupled to the later sets. The London Midland at first began a policy of concentrating them in one area; consequently many of the power-trailers were moved back to North Wales and later to Northwich, before eventually settling to a home at Macclesfield. However, in January 1958 the Light Weight Trains Committee was being told that the five power-twins were surplus to requirements and it was suggested that they should be converted into power-trailers, which would involve removing the engines and transmissions from the Motor Composites and fitting them with replacement bogies. This plan was agreed by

Above: One of the routes that was regularly operated in the Manchester area by the Derby Lightweights was that to Hayfield from Manchester (London Road). A four-car set takes the left-hand road at New Mills Junction, heading for Hayfield.
Kenneth Field, Rail Archive Stephenson

Right: Crossing the Thame Valley near Reddish Junction, this four-car set, made up of two two-car Derby Lightweights, is working to Hayfield.
Kenneth Field, Rail Archive Stephenson

the Carriage & Wagon Engineer at Derby, who suggested reusing the recovered components on new-build units. This would cost £19,100 but there would be a credit of £26,100 for the parts recovered, so the conversion would generate a surplus of £7,000. While a decision was reached, the units were redeployed on the Liverpool-St Helens services, so once the go-ahead was given they

could not be released for conversion. By February 1959 authority was being sought for two power-twin sets to be retained for North Wales services, and this was agreed, but as the bogies for the conversions had already been made two pairs had to be disposed of into spares stock. Accordingly only 79191-93 were actually converted to trailers and were then renumbered 79633-635, spending

Right: A four-car set of Lightweight stock leaves Bredbury, again bound for Hayfield. By the mid-1960s many units had been transferred to Macclesfield, which had become a centre for 'Yellow Diamond'-equipped DMUs. *Kenneth Field, Rail Archive Stephenson*

Below: Pictured at Hagues Park, between New Mills and Strines on the original Midland Railway route into Manchester, this Derby Lightweight set is heading for Manchester (London Road). Units in the green livery could be found with either black or grey roofs in their later days. *Kenneth Field, Rail Archive Stephenson*

the rest of their lives at Llandudno Junction.

By 1960 the original Lightweight cars had been eliminated from the Manchester No 1 area, although they still appeared in the city due to being allocated to sheds in surrounding districts, but, as in other Regions during the 1960s, service contractions released enough 'Blue Square' units, and the 'Yellow Diamond' Lightweights were declared surplus to requirements and all had gone by 1969, most being broken up by commercial contractors.

Lightweights originally allocated to the Manchester area

Number	Type	Diagram	Lot No	Region	Set	Seats	Weight	Built	Partnered with	Depot
79142	DMBS	633	30246	London Midland	Power-trailer	52	27 tons	July 56	79684	Bury
79171/ 72/74/ 76-80	DMBS	633	30321	London Midland	Power-trailer	52	27 tons	Apr-July 56	79672/73/ 75/77-81	Longsight
79184- 79188	DMBS	633	30324	London Midland	Power-twin	52	27 tons	July-Aug 56	79189- 79193	Longsight
79189- 79193*	DMCL	510	30325	London Midland	Power-twin	9F/ 53S	27 tons	July-Aug 56	79184- 79188	Longsight
79672/ 73/75/ 77-81, 79684	DTCL	511	30322	London Midland	Power-trailer	12F/ 53S	21 tons	Apr-May 56	79171/ 72/74/ 76-80	Longsight
									79142	Bury

79191-79193 converted to 79633-79635 in 1962. Diagrams for Lot 633 and Lot 511 are on pages 66/67

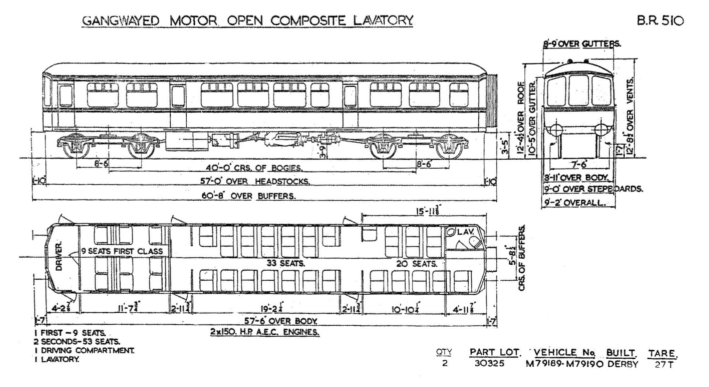

Diagram 510

Left: The short Buxton-Miller's Dale service was turned over to the new railcars on 14 October 1956. One of the Manchester-allocated units is seen here in April 1957 under the impressive overall roof of Buxton station. The middle indicator lamp under the cab has a red lens over it so it can be used as a tail lamp. *N. Sparks, Colour-Rail*

Right: Many of the Lightweights were based at Macclesfield during the mid-1960s. M79665 was originally intended for the Birmingham No 1 scheme, but moved on when the Class 117s were built and was at Macclesfield for several years before withdrawal. A guard fixes the tail lamp at Hayfield station on 30 April 1966. *B. Norman, Colour-Rail*

Left: One Derby Lightweight unit was allocated to Bury to assist the Metro-Cammells based there in working the Bury-Bacup services. However, this power-twin, led by M79192, is not the usual set but is one of the first three power-twins allocated to Longsight Depot. M79192 was eventually converted to a Driving Trailer and renumbered M79634. The set is working the 2.50pm Bury-Bacup service and is seen arriving at Bacup on 1 November 1958. *R. O. Tuck*

13

The single cars

The final two Derby Lightweights to be built to the original design and with diesel engines were unique in that they were fitted with a cab at both ends and were designed for operation as single cars.

At that time a number of feasibility studies had suggested that traffic on lightly used branch lines could be increased by the provision of modern stock, which would also have the effect of lowering operating costs. The former Great Western Railway had had a great deal of success with its fleet of single-car AEC railcars, and it was therefore decided to build single-car units to assess whether there was any merit in provision of such vehicles.

The idea did not come from the Light Weight Trains Committee; in fact, it was merely informed, in April 1956, that an order had been placed by the BTC, but it was asked to comment on it. The Committee observed that a second vehicle would be needed to cover, should the one ordered be unavailable, and that the luggage area was too small. These findings were accepted but it was realised that the first vehicle was already in build and that it was too late to alter the specification at that stage.

The 16-mile-long London Midland Region line between Banbury (Merton Street) and Bletchley via Buckingham was selected for the experiment. Originally planned as a trunk route, the line had, like many others, remained a branch due to competing routes being better

Above: The original arrangements of the radiator filler water pipes and exhausts can be seen clearly in this view of one of the single cars at Water Stratford Halt, heading for Banbury in December 1960. *Colour-Rail*

situated to serve nearby towns and villages. The 1910 service of six trains a day from Bletchley to Buckingham, with four continuing to Banbury, had dropped by 1955 to three between Bletchley and Banbury and four returns. As passenger numbers were insufficient to justify a two-car unit, the line was ideal for the trial.

Official records show that the two vehicles actually came from the original allocation of the Manchester No 1 scheme and, as mentioned previously, it seems likely that a gap in the number series of the Manchester vehicles, comprising 79182 and 79183, arises because the vehicles were altered in the production stage to be fitted with cabs at both ends, and were thus completed as 79900 and 79901.

The first vehicle, M79900, which appeared in September 1956, was built with 61 2nd Class seats, and had two rows of facing seats between the guard's compartment and the rear vestibule. However, because of the second cab, which occupied space at the other end of the compartment, the guard's space was very limited; as a result the second unit, M79901, appeared without these seats and with the guard's bulkhead moved up to the

Above: A works photograph showing the interior of M79900. The 2nd Class upholstery was by this time green with a flower pattern. *British Railways*

vestibule, resembling the internal layout of the London Midland and production North Eastern sets. This vehicle seated only 52 2nd Class passengers. Neither unit had a toilet or 1st Class accommodation. M79900 soon disappeared to have the extra seats removed and the guard's compartment enlarged, but the two vehicles could always be distinguished as the first had a large window at each side where the seating had originally been fitted, while the second had a smaller window in the centre of the guard's compartment.

The mechanical layout was identical to the earlier vehicles, with the same AEC 150hp diesel engines and Wilson gearboxes being fitted. However, the exhausts from the engines had to be taken up the front of the second cab, between the cab windows, and were then joined together at roof level. The front was made even more messy by the additional pipes provided so that the roof-mounted engine water header tanks could be topped up, though these were later removed when the roof tanks were removed and expansion tanks fitted. There was no view forward for the passengers when the train was being driven from the No 2 (guard's compartment) end, as both ends of the compartment had solid walls. Both cars were allocated to Bletchley (1E).

The service between Banbury and Buckingham started on 13 August 1956, two additional halts were opened on the line, and the new single cars cut operating costs by a third. Revenue increased fourfold, cutting annual losses from £14,000 to £4,700, but this was still not enough to satisfy British Railways, which noted that traffic was still sparse, except for market days. Even less impressed was Lord Rusholme, Chairman of the British Transport Commission, who visited the line during the first week of 1957 and concluded in a memo (1) that the line could never pay, (2) that business could never justify the services, (3) that the area was well served by buses, and (4) that the stations were too far away from the villages. He further decreed that the service could continue for 12 months, but if there was no dramatic improvement it should be closed down; meanwhile no more halts were to be constructed.

The improved passenger numbers never came and, despite a lot of last-minute objections and wrangling, services were cut back to Buckingham on 2 January 1961. The single cars continued to work the eight-trains-a-day service on this stub until 7 September 1964, when this part of the branch was also axed, rendering them surplus to requirements.

Left: The second single car, M79901, is captured at Bletchley on 22 August 1964. The small window to serve the guard's van can be seen, which makes this unit easy to tell apart from its sister. *Alec Swain, www.transporttreasury.co.uk*

When the branch had originally been proposed for closure, the two new single-car units would have been an attractive proposition to another Region, and in fact the London Midland did discuss with the BTC in June 1958 the possible transfer of the two to the Buxton-Miller's Dale branch in Derbyshire, but by the time of the actual closure there were sufficient two-car units in Manchester to cover the services and the area had already actively tried to rid itself of its 'Yellow Diamond' units.

M79901 was taken out of capital stock in December 1966 and cut up at Bletchley in April 1967, when only 12 years and 5 months old, but its sister was shown as briefly allocated to York before it, too, was withdrawn in October 1967. Happily this was not to be the end, for this vehicle was taken into departmental service and became one of the first to be allocated to the British Railways Technical Centre at Derby, where it was renumbered RDB975010. Here it received a number of modifications, including the fitting of a toilet compartment and a large mains generator. Once again full-height pipes appeared on the No 2 driving end, though this time these were to fill up the toilet water tank that had been installed in the roof. The exhausts were also modified so that they were completely independent of each other. The seating was removed so that test equipment could be housed, mostly in the central compartment.

Incredibly, M79900, in its new guise and known as *Iris*, was to be very long-lived as it was used for experimental work that included into the provision of Electronic Token Block Signalling and Driver Only Radio. In this capacity it travelled the length and breadth of the country, usually under its own power, testing signal strengths and taking part in other experiments. By the mid-1990s it had already been in departmental service for more than 30 years and, as a sign of its historical importance, was repainted into a version of the British Railways green livery. It was finally withdrawn in 1999 and, fortunately already stripped of asbestos, was immediately preserved, being taken to the Midland Railway-Butterley in running order. There complete restoration to original condition was undertaken; the generator and toilet compartment were removed, the guard's bulkhead relocated and the passenger seats refitted. The unit was also rewired to the 'Blue Square' system, as it was then the only surviving vehicle with the 'Yellow Diamond' coupling system, and it can now work with all other surviving first-generation multiple units.

Following initial service at Butterley and visits to other heritage railways at Llangollen and Cheddleton, M79900 was transferred to the Ecclesbourne Valley Railway at Wirksworth, where it continues in service.

Derby Lightweight single cars

Numbers	Type	Diagram	Lot No	Seats	Introduced	To
M79900	DMBS (single car)	514	30380	61S	July 56	1E Bletchley
M79901	DMBS (single car)	515	30387	52S	Aug 56	1E Bletchley

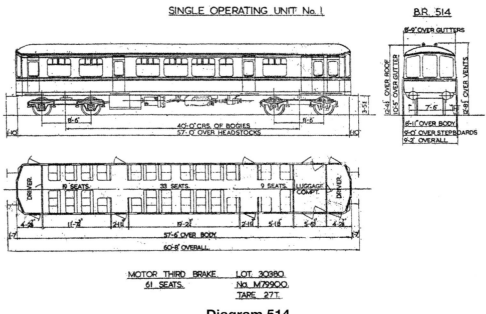

Diagram 514

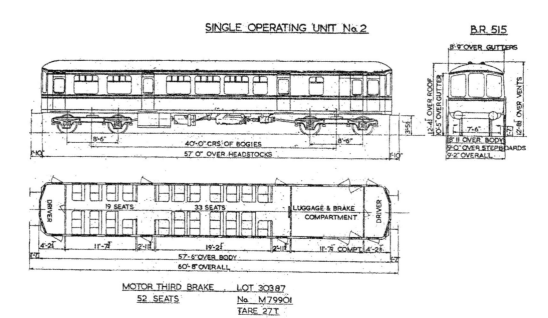

SINGLE OPERATING UNIT No. 2

B.R. 515

Diagram 515

MOTOR THIRD BRAKE . LOT 30387
52 SEATS   No. M79901
                  TARE 27T

Left: The two single cars often worked coupled together. Here they are seen at Blunham; M79900, with its larger guard's window, is nearest the camera. *Colour-Rail*

Left: Both of the singles are working together again in this picture, taken on 27 October 1956, and have arrived at Buckingham from Banbury. As usual there are not many passengers. *S. Creer*

Above: The second-built car, M79901, is seen at Fulwell & Westbury on 23 July 1957 working the 11.05am Banbury to Bletchley service. *M. G. D. Farr*

Above right: Passengers were denied a driver's-eye view at the guard's end of the units, as can be seen in this photograph, of M79901, at Banbury (Merton Street) on 15 July 1959. *M. G. D. Farr*

Middle: Banbury (Merton Street) was a dismal run-down station that even the new single cars could do nothing to improve. Both cars are seen waiting to work the 1.55pm service to Buckingham on 10 December 1960. *Leslie Sandler*

Bottom: The first unit went on to have a long and successful departmental career and is seen here on 14 March 1987 passing Smitham en route from Tattenham Corner to Pig Hill Sidings, near Clapham Junction, while engaged on Southern Region radio tests. *David Brown*

14

The battery-electric Lightweight

The final Derby Lightweight set made an appearance in March 1958, being a special one-off for the Aberdeen-Ballater branch in Scotland.

However, unlike all the earlier vehicles, this set was not fitted with diesel engines but was instead constructed to take its power from a large bank of batteries, which were fitted to the DMBS where the engines were usually located and in a similar position between the bogies on what would have been the trailer car. These fed electric traction motors, which drove the train.

The concept of a train driven by batteries was not new; the first had been introduced by Witfield on the Palatine Railway in 1896 and examples had been tried in the USA as early as 1911. There were many disadvantages, particularly with the provision of batteries of sufficient power and their limited range, but there were considerable advantages, including a low operating cost, lack of pollution and quiet running.

Many areas of Scotland were provided with hydro-electric power stations that generated electricity at a cost-effective rate, and as early as 1954 the North of Scotland Hydro-Electric Board had suggested to the British Transport Commission that some of this power might be usefully provided for train propulsion purposes. Detailed investigation suggested to the BTC that there would be no financial advantages, but this conclusion was

Above: The battery-electric unit can easily be identified due to the battery boxes between the bogies. Other differences included the lack of electrical jumper cables or vacuum pipes at the vehicle ends. The ventilator grille below the centre cab window also seems to have disappeared during the conversion process. *C. Lawson Kerr*

challenged in the House of Commons with the result that in 1956 the BTC gave an undertaking to carry out an experiment in the use of battery-operated railcars on a branch line in Scotland. Those supporting the project hoped that the cheaper running costs of the battery train would result in the retention of lines that would otherwise be threatened with closure.

By the following May a pair of complete Derby Lightweight vehicles had been delivered to St Rollox Works in Glasgow. At this stage they were not fitted with any form of underfloor equipment, apart from the bogies. It seems likely that the two vehicles, a DMBS and a DTC, were not specially built for the scheme but were added to the production of vehicles being built at Derby, as the bodies were identical in every way to standard vehicles.

Both cars were then fitted with very large battery cradles in between the two bogies, which contained a total of 216 lead acid cells, creating current at 440V and 1,070amp/hours, and for which additional strengthening was required. These fed control equipment, which was mostly housed in the guard's compartment area and was provided by Siemens-Schuckert and Schaltbau to the same pattern as had been provided for a number of successful battery-electric railcars operating in Germany. Power was taken to the wheels of the DMBS via two 100kW traction motors, which were mounted on one bogie.

Unlike all the other Lightweight DMUs the battery-electric set was equipped with air brakes, rather than vacuum, the power for which came from an electrically driven compressor mounted in the driving trailer. The control for this was placed in the same place as the vacuum brake on a normal unit. Other changes to the controls included the elimination of the gear lever, which was not required, and the removal of the direction selector to the left-hand side of the cab, where it was amalgamated with the power controller. A larger than usual instrument panel was provided, which contained the speedometer, voltmeter and ammeter, with the engine speed indicator being deleted.

The ends of the two cars were not fitted with jumper cables, nor air or vacuum pipes, as the vehicle's control system meant that it was not compatible with any other multiple unit, or indeed train.

An official announcement that construction of a battery-electric train was under way was made by Sir Ian Bolton, Chairman of the Scottish Area Board of the BTC, at a press conference in Glasgow on 15 October 1957. Sir Ian confirmed that the new train would be used on the Aberdeen-Ballater branch, which would see its daily services increased from four to six, half of which would be worked by the new battery unit. Delivery of the new unit was promised for the summer of 1958.

In the event the battery-electric railcar was ready for its launch earlier than that, and a special trip for the press took place on Wednesday 26 March 1958. This was also attended by representatives from the BTC, the Hydro-Electric Board, British Railways, local councils and businessmen. A party of 117 people travelled one way from Ballater to Aberdeen and the event was a complete success.

Following staff training, regular services began on Monday 21 April and steam passenger work was eliminated from the branch from July, when a standard Metro-Cammell Class 101 DMU arrived to work the second diagram.

The Ballater line was 43 miles in length, and had 12 intermediate stations. Gradients were as steep as 1 in 70, which would require high power output from the batteries. However, experience with the German trains had shown that 100-150 miles was perfectly feasible between battery charging. High-capacity battery chargers were installed at both Ballater and Aberdeen and the diagrams for the unit were organised in such a way that there were 50-60-minute layovers after each journey, which could be used to partially recharge the system.

The battery-electric settled down to largely reliable service, with very few failures recorded against it, and was initially outstabled at Ballater, moving to Aberdeen in 1960. The train was said to be very smooth and quiet and popular with passengers. In 1962 it was equipped with a new set of improved batteries, but it lasted only a few more months in service after this and was initially withdrawn in August 1962. There were periodic returns to service in the years that followed, but by that time the Beeching Report had identified the branch as one of those that was to be closed, with the axe finally falling on passenger traffic on 28 February 1966 and on goods on 30 December of the same year. The battery-electric was withdrawn from capital stock in the same month and was placed in store at Cowlairs.

Right: This intriguing picture shows the battery-electric unit apparently complete, but a closer look reveals that there is no underframe equipment or batteries fitted. Presumably the picture was taken after the vehicles had been completed at Derby Works but before the traction equipment was fitted at Cowlairs. *British Railways*

Fortunately this would not be the end for this unique train, as it was claimed by the Railway Technical Centre in 1967 and taken to Derby, from where it was used for British Rail Automatic Train Operation tests, being fitted with experimental train-mounted equipment. Renumbered RDB975003 and RDB975004, and nicknamed 'Gemini', the set was usually based at Mickleover and operated on the Mickleover-Egginton Junction line. The green livery previously carried (which had never had any form of 'speed whisker' or yellow panel added) gave way to a red/blue livery in the style of the blue/grey livery then being applied to main-line coaches, and a buffer beam air pipe was added. The RTC used the set for 17 years before finally deciding that it had no further use for it, and it was put up for sale in 1984, by which time it was two of only five Derby Lightweight vehicles still in existence.

The battery-electric was subsequently purchased by the West Yorkshire Transport Museum, which was seeking to establish a major museum on the site of Low Moor Station, near Bradford – a scheme that would have seen a section of line between there and Heckmondwike reopened for the benefit of visitors. Taken initially to Bradford Hammerton Street Depot, ironically the depot to which the first of the Derby Lightweights had been allocated, a considerable sum of money was spent in the removal of asbestos insulation and a subsequent rebuild. However, when the museum finally opened it did so without the promised heritage ride and, as a result, the battery-electric set was loaned to the East Lancashire Railway around 1994. There its refurbishment was completed and it was repainted into British Railways green once again.

Unfortunately the West Yorkshire Transport Museum subsequently went out of business and the battery-electric was offered for sale by the liquidators, who eventually came to an agreement with the fledgling Royal Deeside Railway project, which took delivery of the unit in 2001. Used as loco-hauled stock, the set is now based at Milton on Crathes, a station on the original Aberdeen-Ballater line for which the unit was originally designed.

Above: Inside Sc79999's 1st Class area 12 seats were provided, upholstered in blue moquette, similar to the green pattern used in 2nd Class. *British Railways*

Battery-electric set

Numbers	Type	Diagram	Lot No	Seats	Introduced	To
Sc79998	DMBS	406	30368	52S	Mar 58	61A Aberdeen (Ballater)
Sc79999	DMC	442	30369	12F/53S	Mar 58	As above

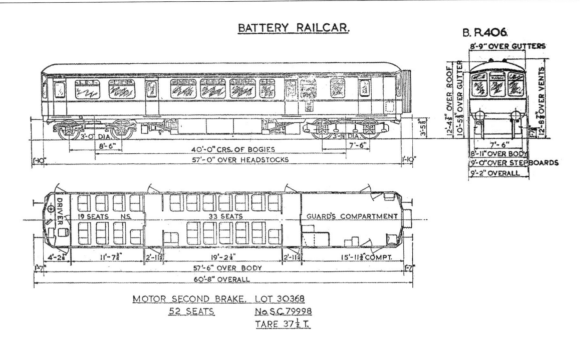

Diagram 406

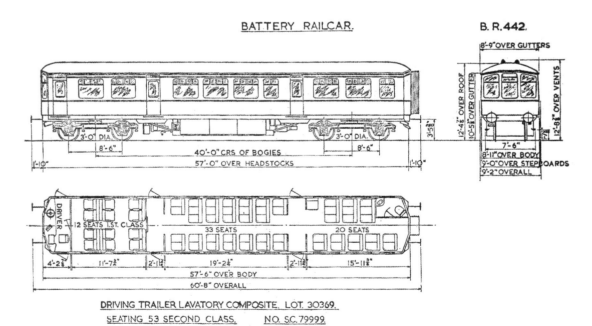

Diagram 442

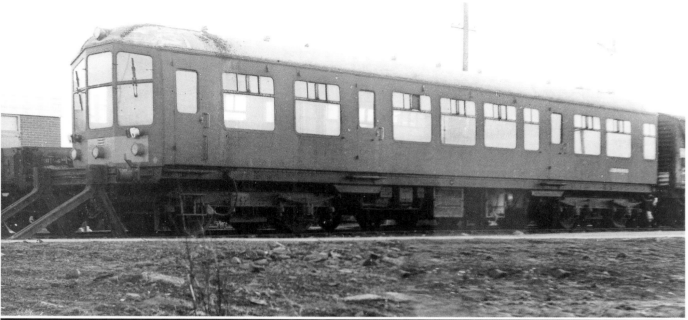

15

The oddball – the saloon Lightweight

Some years after the final first series of Derby Lightweights came off the production line, there appeared a novel and interesting conversion of an existing unit that came about due to a perceived requirement for an independently powered saloon that could be used for official visits by railway officers.

In November 1956 the Chairman of the British Transport Commission, Sir Brian Robertson, made an official visit to the Holyhead, Crewe and Manchester areas. To make his inspection more comfortable, an almost new two-car Derby unit was taken out of traffic and the trailer was modified with a number of temporary fittings to make it suitable for official use. The trailer chosen for this prestigious duty was 79649, which had been built originally for the Birmingham No 1 scheme but had soon gravitated to North Wales as more 'Blue Square' units had become available.

The trip was, by all accounts, a great success, and David Blee, the General Manager at Euston, enquired whether there was likely to be any money available for the construction of a permanent new two-car saloon, but the proposal was declined. There matters seemed to rest for a considerable period until the Carriage & Wagon Department at Derby realised that there was, in fact, one spare similar trailer car, 79683, which had been originally allocated to Llandudno Junction and which was under-used.

Above: One Derby Lightweight trailer was converted into a saloon for use on the London Midland Region. Although M79649 retained its original number for some time, it had been renumbered to 999510 when pictured stored at Carstairs on 27 March 1975. *D. L. Percival*

It seems that the opportunity was then taken to match 79683 with 79649's power car to make a complete set for passenger service, thus releasing 79649 for saloon use. For this purpose the interior was extensively modified – the centre section was fitted with a large table that could seat ten, together with a desk and a cocktail cabinet, while the small saloon at the rear was fitted with two wardrobes, food storage area, a sink and a hot-water heater. The former 1st Class area, which had 12 seats, remained untouched. At some point the vehicle was also modified to have 'Blue Square' electrics, although when this occurred is not clear.

By 1959 the saloon was in regular use and A. E. Robson, Chief Mechanical & Electrical Engineer, London Midland Region, raised the subject of its poor seating, asking if better seats could be fitted at the observation ends, though this was not carried out, as to provide seats at the end of the standard power car, which was 'borrowed' each time the saloon was required, would render it useless for ordinary services. A few months later the provision of a replacement new two-car saloon was discussed, at which time it was estimated that it would cost around £3,000 to return 79649 to normal configuration. An inventory of items that would be declared surplus should this happen was, however, prepared, and this showed that a fixed table, dining room chairs, lined curtains, sink unit, cupboard, cocktail cabinet and stove would have to be removed. In 1962 authority was sought for the purchase of six revolving chairs to

replace the original 1st Class seats, and these were fitted in 1963 at a cost of £473. By this time the trailer had been renumbered DB999510 and placed permanently in the departmental fleet.

It seems to have spent much of its life parked at various places and is shown as officially withdrawn in 1981, easily outliving most of the others from the same series; it met its end at Mayer Newman of Snailwell.

The saloon Lightweight

Number	Type	Diagram	Lot No	Set	Seats	Weight	Converted	Partnered when new	Original depot
999510 (79649)	Saloon	565	30241	Power-trailer		23 tons	1959	As required	Derby HQ

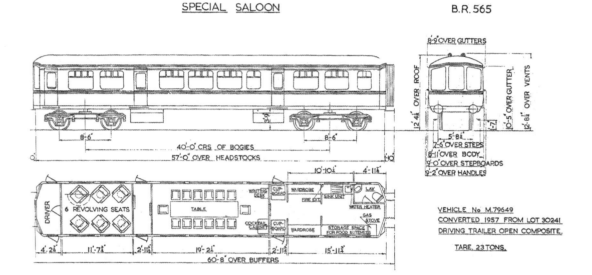

Diagram 565

16

Operational experiences

G iven that the Derby Lightweight vehicles were designed and the initial vehicles produced over a remarkably short period of only 15 months – and that those building them had little experience with the type – it has to be said that it is surprising that there were so few major faults.

The decision to use light alloy was as a result of the limited power available from the 125hp Leyland engine, and, as has been related, once the 150hp power units were available it was possible to build in steel, at a considerable cost saving. The Derby Lightweights suffered from a number of structural weaknesses in consequence of being built of light alloy that were eradicated on later designs, such as the first Metro-Cammells.

Early Derby-built cars soon exhibited a tendency to suffer damage to the headstocks and ends, even when involved in fairly minor heavy shunts, and a modification to the design soon saw cars built with steel headstocks and with the rivets between the ends of the vehicles and the bogie centres changed from light alloy to steel to increase strength. Older vehicles were rebuilt as required and most underwent this during their lifetime. Because of this weakness quite a few of the Derby Lightweights were written off as a result of collisions; in January 1965, for instance, a South Gosforth-allocated set, DMBS E79139 and DTC E79659, was condemned after what was officially described as a 'mishap'.

Above: This very unusual shot shows a Blaenau branch service near Pont-y-Pant with passengers disembarking because of what the photographer noted was a broken axle on the rear bogie of the second coach. The picture is dated 22 July 1962. *Colour-Rail*

It was also found that the bodies had a tendency to sag when under heavy load and that once this happened the doors would jam shut; this caused an initial ban on more than 100 people being carried in each coach. The problem was eradicated by providing a strengthening piece below each door opening, a design feature that was carried onto all subsequent Derby Lightweight builds. There were also problems at the gangway ends where the soft alloy was soon worn away by the actions of the corridor connection; this was solved by fitting a steel member on which the connection could rub.

Also problematical were the large windscreens fitted to the West Riding and Cumberland sets, which proved susceptible to damage and further weakened the ends of the cars. From the Lincolnshire sets onwards the design was modified so that the windscreens were split in two by a horizontal body member just above the driver's head. Cars from the first two batches subsequently received a strengthening bar behind the glass but retained the full-height screen. On all but the first two batches the windscreen wiper, which had previously been mounted to one side of the windscreen, was relocated on the windscreen dividing member.

The inherent weakness of the design showed up later in the Derby vehicles' lives when the class began to suffer from fatigue fractures in the main underframe members in the areas where the engines and gearboxes were mounted. The cure for this was to splice in replacement steel sections, which was an extremely expensive exercise as it involved removing all the underfloor equipment to gain access to the affected areas. On the positive side, the bodies did not suffer from corrosion and most were in excellent order when they were withdrawn.

Both the Derby Lightweights and the early Metro-Cammells were fitted with a bogie based in that originally designed for the Liverpool-Southport electric stock, which was designed for stock running at a maximum speed of 60mph. However, at the higher speeds operated

This page and opposite: This interesting sequence of photos shows E79622, originally a Lincoln vehicle but later transferred to East Anglia, having repairs at Derby Works after a heavy shunt. The buffer beam has broken away and the main frame has bent. Repairs of this magnitude were common due to the structural weaknesses of the Derby Lightweights. As can be seen, steel was used in the repair, and a new buffer beam and frame main members were grafted on to the vehicle. *British Railways*

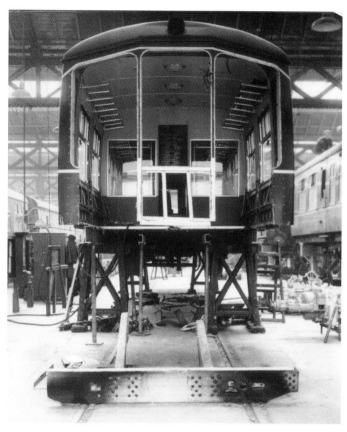

by the new railcars riding became rather rough, and this was eventually traced to the inclined swing links, which were quite short and mounted at an angle, and also to the stiffness of the bolster springs. The bogies were progressively modified to include longer, vertically mounted swing links, and softer bolster springs were fitted, which allowed a smoother ride. Despite these modifications, most of the first-generation units remained quite lively at speed, with a tendency to roll around on jointed track. There were also problems with axle failures, which were cured by changing to a larger axle end diameter. Early on in their life, in October 1955, the West Cumberland sets were reported as suffering excessive wheel wear; 79010 had to be returned to Derby, having covered only 48,201 miles from new. Changes to the way the brake rigging was set up apparently cured this problem, with no further instances being reported.

One of the biggest issues with the early Derby cars was the arrangement of the water system for the engine. The original design provided for the header and expansion tanks to be mounted on the roofs with water pipes passing down to the engines beneath. There was no radiator level gauge and considerable amounts of water were lost through expansion, or through the effects of a train going up and down gradients. Obviously there were lengthy pipe runs and many joints involved with this system, all of which were potential causes of leaks. It was also found that steam pockets were developing in the water system due to there being insufficient capacity for it to absorb water displaced by expansion. Consequently the radiator system was redesigned to incorporate a header tank and an expansion tank, which were mounted in the saloon, under the seats, all of the pipework and tanks on the roofs then being done away with. The system was also pressurised to 5psi at this time. When the specifications were drawn up for outside companies to build their versions of the railcars, these changes were specified from new, so the Metro-Cammell vehicles never had the roof-mounted expansion tanks.

Although the gearboxes were to a proven design there were problems in the early days with severe wear of the brake bands. It was thought that this was due to some drivers changing gear without allowing time for the gearbox brake drums to come to rest. Consequently in 1957 one of the North Wales-allocated lightweights, M79135, was fitted with an automatic gear-changing system. The unit retained its Wilson gearbox and a system was devised that used magnets to pick up the speeds of the gearbox. This was not developed further, though similar systems were tried later on other types of car, and the experimental vehicle was returned to standard configuration. The problem was then alleviated, though not cured, by better driver training.

A problem common to all of the early DMUs was the failure of the reversing mechanism in the final drive. Originally, when changing direction, drivers were asked to stop the engines, which ensured there was as little force as possible on the fork, which moved the reversing gear from one side to the other. After complaints from the operating departments about the time this took, the instruction was modified to allow a change of direction with the engines running. Unfortunately this triggered a massive increase in failures, which took some time to rectify; strengthened forks, new bronze change-over pistons and twin air seals were gradually introduced to overcome the problem.

Despite the fact that the provision of adequate heating had been such an issue at the design stage, the Smith's oil-fired heaters proved reliable in service. Unfortunately the early cars were fitted with only one heater of 40,000BthU/hr, and were found to be impossibly cold in winter. As a result later builds were equipped with two heaters of 50,000BthU/hr each, but the Lightweight cars all remained fitted with one each until the end.

Although the West Riding sets were equipped with generators that charged the batteries all the time the engines were running, these were found to be unsatisfactory because the engines spent so much of their time idling. The generators were de-rated and altered to work over a larger speed range, but there were still a large number of flat batteries. The Cumberland sets were equipped with dynamos driven off the engines by means of a belt, but this also proved unsatisfactory, so later vehicles were produced with conventional high-output coach generators, driven by belt from the drive shafts, which worked only when the train was doing above 15mph. While these were much more successful they did not solve the problem totally, but the Derby Lightweight and Metro-Cammell cars retained this system until the end.

The electrical system was rated at 24 volts, the same as on loco-hauled coaches, and the control system was organised in such a way that operation of the cab controls provided power to electro-pneumatic valves, which in turn allowed air to operate the throttle, gears and reversing mechanisms. The system worked well when controlling just the two sets of equipment on each power car but it was found that when sets were coupled together in multiple there was sufficient voltage drop through the train wires to cause erratic or sluggish operation of components in following sets. The solution to this was to redesign the control system so that each car took power from its own batteries via relays and acted on an electrical command from the train wires. Derby Lightweight and Metro-Cammell cars could have been rewired to comply with the later system (and budgets for this were prepared), but in view of the contraction of the railway system this work was never done and the units were withdrawn instead. Until then traffic was organised in such a way that the early units worked grouped together on specific work or in specific areas. The early control system became known as 'Yellow Diamond' and the later one 'Blue Square', with the latter becoming the standard.

Conclusion

Both the Derby Lightweights and the early Metro-Cammells proved to be a significant success and achieved the objectives that their designers and advocates had set out for them.

In fact, so spectacular were the results that the British Transport Commission had soon ordered more than 4,000 diesel multiple unit trains, which transformed the face of British Railways. Literally thousands of steam locomotives, some little more than a few years old, were rendered surplus and countless carriages were also consigned to scrap.

However, despite the reductions in running costs, many of the lines modernised were saddled with expensive infrastructure, which included high levels of staff at stations. The rise in the popularity, and affordability, of the private car in the late 1950s and early 1960s severely impacted on passenger numbers and many passengers were lost to road transport in this period.

Even before Dr Beeching wielded his famous axe, rationalisation of unprofitable lines was taking place. Routes that had their stations inconveniently sited for the villages and towns they were supposed to serve, or which had been built in areas where the population was small, were the first to be badly affected.

As a result, once British Railways had got rid of all the steam engines it found itself in a situation where it had a surplus of trains and a system that was continuing to

contract. Of all the units then in service, only the Derby Lightweights and the early Metro-Cammells (with the exception of a handful of parcels units) had the 'Yellow Diamond' coupling system, which led to problems when they had to interact with other types of units. In addition, the structural problems of the Derby Lightweights were proving to be something of a liability. A policy therefore began of reallocating 'Blue Square' units from areas suffering closures to those equipped with the 'Yellow Diamond' machines. Cumberland received batches of the later Derby Lightweights (Class 108s), for instance, while East Anglia received substantial numbers of the later Metro-Cammells (Class 101).

Once these reallocations were completed by the late 1960s, there was not enough work to go round and it was obvious that there never would be, so although both classes were relatively modern, the decision was taken to scrap them.

In view of the new technology that these trains represented to mainland UK, the fact that they worked at all was remarkable. That they worked so well and proved a suitable base from which all subsequent types could be developed was nothing short of extraordinary. Many of the initial design errors were corrected fairly quickly in subsequent batches of the Derby Lightweights, while the Metro-Cammells had the benefit of British Railways' experience with the Derby vehicles, enabling them to build a reliable product from the start.

Had the railways not contracted so suddenly it is likely that both classes would have given many more years of service. As it was, all met an early end, but paved the way for a complete revolution that has seen diesel multiple unit trains become the predominant mode of traction on Britain's railways.

Derby Lightweights

Number	Type	Diagram	Lot. No	Region	Set	Seats	Weight	Built	No Cars	Partnered new	Original Depot	Withdrawn
79000-79007	DMBS	501	30084	Eastern (West Riding)	P Twin	61	26t	4.54-9.54	2	79500-79507	Bradford Hammerton Street	1964
79008-79020	DMBS	503	30123	Midland (Cumberland)	P Twin	61	27t	11.54-1.55	2	79600-79612	Carlisle	1967/8
79021-79033	DMBS	504	30126	Eastern (Lincs)	P Trailer	56	27t	1.55-6.55	2	79613-79625	Lincoln	1968
79034-79046	DMBS	504	30177	Eastern (East Anglia)	P Trailer	56	27t	6.55- 8.55	2	79250-79262	Norwich	1961-1968
79118-79126	DMBS	633	30235	Midland	P Trailer	52	27t	11.55-1.56	2	79639-79647	Monument Lane	1965-1969
79127-79134 79135-79136	DMBS	633	30240	Midland N.Wales	P Trailer	52	27t	2.56-3.56	2	79648-79655 79656-79657	Monument Lane Llandudno Junct	1967-1969
79137-79140	DMBS	527	30240	Eastern (Newcastle)	P Trailer	52	27t	3.56	2	79658-79661	South Gosforth	1963-1968
79141 79142	DMBS	633	30246	Midland	P Trailer	52	27t	4.56-7.56	2	79662 79684	Monument Lane Bury	1967-1969
79143-79149	DMBS	633	30201	Midland	P Trailer	52	27t	1.56-2.56	2	79663-79669	Monument Lane	1967-1969
79150-79154	DMS	518	30193	Eastern (Newcastle)	4-car	64	27t	9.55	4	79325-79329 79400-79404 79508-79512	South Gosforth	1966-1967
79169-79170 79171-79181 #	DMBS	633	30321	Midland	P Trailer	52	27t	4.56-7.56	2	79670-79671 79672-79682	Monument Lane Llandudno Junct	1961/7 1967-9
79184-79188	DMBS	633	30324	Midland (Manchester)	P Twin	52	27t	7.56-8.56	2	79189-79193	Longsight	1964-1969
79189-79193 *	DMCL	510	30325	Midland (Manchester)	P Twin	9/53	27t	7.56-8.56	2	79184-79188	Longsight	1967-1969
79250-79262	DTCL	505	30128	Eastern (East Anglia)	P Trailer	16/53	21t	7.55-8.55	2	79034-79046	Norwich	1967-1968
79325-79329	TBSL	508	30194	Eastern (Newcastle)	4-car	45	21t	9.55	4	79150-79154 79400-79404 79508-79512	South Gosforth	1966-1967
79400-79404	TSL	517	30195	Eastern (Newcastle)	4-car	61	21t	9.55	4	79508-79512 79325-79329 79150-79154	South Gosforth	1966-1967
79500-79507	DMCL	507	30085	Eastern (West Riding)	P Twin	16/53	27t	4.54-9.54	2	79000-79007	Bradford Hamm St.	1964
79508-79512	DMC	502	30192	Eastern (Newcastle)	4-car	20/36	27t	9.55	4	79325-79329 79400-79404 79150-79154	South Gosforth	1966-1967
79600-79612	DTCL	509	30124	Midland (Cumberland)	P Trailer	9/53	21t	11.54-1.55	2	79008-79020	Carlisle	1968
79613-79625	DTCL	505	30127	Eastern (Lincs)	P Trailer	16/53	21t	1.55-5.55	2	79021-79033	Lincoln	1962-1968
79633-79635 (former nos 79191-93)	DTCL	509	30325	Midland (North Wales)	P Trailer	9/53	21t	Converted 5.62	2		Llandudno Junct	1969
79639-79647	DTCL	509	30236	Midland	P Trailer	9/53	21t	11.55-1.56	2	79118-79126	Monument Lane	1968-1969
79648-79655 79656-79657	DTCL	509	30241	Midland	P Trailer	9/53	21t	2.56-3.56	2	79127-79134 79135-79136	Monument Lane Llandudno Junction	1967-1969
79658-79661	DTCL	631	30241	Eastern (Newcastle)	P Trailer	16/53	21t	3.56	2	79137-79140	South Gosforth	1963-1968
79662	DTCL	642	30247	Midland	P Trailer	12/53	21t	4.56	2	79141	Monument Lane	1967
79663-79669	DTCL	642	30202	Midland	P Trailer	12/53	21t	1.56-2.56	2	79143-79149	Monument Lane	1967-1969
79670-79671 79672-79682 79683 79684	DTCL	511	30322	Midland	P Trailer	12/53	21t	4.56-5.56	2	79169- 79170 79171-79181 Spare 79142	Monument Lane Llandudno Junction Bury	1967-1969
79900	DMBS	514	30380	Midland	Single	61	27t	7.56	1	n/a	Bletchley	1968
79901	DMBS	515	30387	Midland	Single	52	27t	8.56	1	n/a	Bletchley	1968
79998	DMBS	406	30368	Scottish	Battery Electric	52	37 tons 10cwt	03.58	2	79999	Ballater	1966
79999	DTC	442	30369	Scottish	Battery Electric	12F 53S	32 tons 10cwt	03.58	2	79998	Ballater	1966

Notes

Note that DMBS Nos 79182-3 were never issued. As these were part of the original Manchester allocation, from which the two vehicles for the Bletchley scheme were taken while in production it is likely that they were actually completed as 79900 and 79901.

* 79191-79193 were originally DMCs but were converted to DTs 79633-35 in 1962

Metro-Cammell Lightweights

Number	Type	Diagram	Lot. No	Region	Set	Seats	Weight	Built	No Cars	Partnered new	Original Depot	Withdrawn
79047-79056 79057-79058 79059-79064 79065-79066 79067-79075	DMBS	591	30190	Eastern	Power Trailer	56	26t 10cwt	01.56-08.56	2	79263-79272 79273-79274 79275-79280 79281-79282 79283-79291	Norwich Stratford Lincoln Norwich Lincoln	1968- 1969
79076-79082	DMBS	592	30190	Midland (Bury)	Power Trailer	52	26t 10cwt	12.55	2	79626-79632	Bury	1964-1967
79263-79272 79273-79274 79275-79280 79281-79282 79283-79291	DTS	593	30191	Eastern	Power Trailer	72	25 tons	01.56-08.56	2	79047-79056 79057-79058 79059-79064 79065-79066 79067-79075	Norwich Stratford Lincoln Norwich Lincoln	1968- 1969
79626-79632	DTC	594	30191	Midland (Bury)	Power Trailer	12F 53S	25 tons	12.55	2	79076-79082	Bury	1967